Not your Grandma's crochet

Not your Grandma's crochet

EASY CROCHET CLOTHES YOU ACTUALLY WANT TO WEAR

Beth Povey

Contents

Chilled and comfy
007

- 010 **Skill Builder: Making sense of patterns**
- 012 **Coaster**
- 016 **Bookmark**
- 020 **Granny squares & stripes cardigan**
- 032 **Raglan short-sleeved jumper**

Out and about in the city
043

- 046 **Skill Builder: Essential crochet stitches**
- 050 **Granny stripe collar**
- 056 **Grandad's vest**
- 068 **Love heart scrunchie**
- 072 **Retro flower bag**

All out summer holiday
079

- 082 **Skill Builder: Changing yarn colour**
- 084 **Sunglasses case**
- 088 **Summer flower top hat**
- 094 **Hold my ruffle bag**
- 100 **Daisy chain bag**

Cosy winter vibes
109

- 112 **Skill Builder: Finishing your pieces**
- 114 **Retro flower scarf**
- 120 **Retro flower jumper**
- 134 **Mittens**
- 140 **The Wally hat**

Festival ready
141

- 148 **Skill Builder: Joining pieces together/joining as you go**
- 152 **Mini skirt**
- 160 **Checked flower vest**
- 172 **Granny square hat**
- 178 **Granny squares cross body bag**

- 184 *Index*
- 188 *Thank you*

These patterns are all about comfort. Settle in with a cup of tea on your crocheted coaster, while reading a book with your crocheted bookmark and wearing a cosy cardigan or jumper.

Chilled and comfy

SKILL BUILDER

Making sense of the patterns

U.K TO U.S CROCHET TERMS

The patterns in the book use U.K terms, however U.S terms are not the same. Here is a table to show how to convert the stitches.

U.K	U.S
Slip Knot	Slip Knot
Slip stitch (ss)	Slip stitch (ss)
Chain (ch)	Chain (ch)
Double crochet (dc)	Single crochet (sc)
Half treble crochet (htr)	Half double crochet (hdc)
Treble crochet (tr)	Double crochet (dc)
Double treble crochet (dtr)	Treble crochet (tr)
Double crochet 2 together (dc2tog)	Single crochet 2 together (sc2tog)
Treble crochet 2 together (tr2tog)	Double crochet 2 together (dc2tog)
Front post treble crochet (fptr)	Front post double crochet (fpdc)

Tension/Gauge

It is super important to get your tension correct. If you do not, the size of the piece and the amount of yarn needed will be affected. It may feel time consuming to make a gauge swatch but it can save you A LOT of time in the long run.

A gauge swatch is a sample square made with your chosen yarn and the stitch used in the pattern to create the fabric. Everyone's tension is different, so to check if your tension is correct for the pattern you need to make a gauge swatch. To make a gauge swatch, look at the pattern to find out what hook size and stitch is needed. Usually tension/gauge is measured in 10cm X 10cm square but I would always recommend making your swatch bigger (12-15cm) as this will give you a more accurate swatch. Once your gauge swatch is complete, lay it out flat and measure how many stitches and rows are in 10cm x 10cm (or the measurements the pattern shows). If you have the right amount of stitches that's great! If the amount of stitches are less than what is stated, go up a hook size; if the number of stitches is more, go down a hook size. Repeat the swatching process until you have the right tension.

Sizing

All the patterns in this book show you how to make sizes XS–5XL. To find the best size for you, measure around the fullest part of your bust/chest. Use the table in the pattern to find which size will work best for you. If the design is a tight-fitting piece but you would prefer it to be more oversized, go up a size or two and vice versa.

SKILL LEVEL

Coaster

These coasters make the perfect gift. They are quick and pretty easy to make!

You will need:
- 3mm hook (or corresponding hook to reach gauge)
- Dk yarn – approx 20g

Recommended yarn
Paintbox Yarns, Cotton, Dk

Yarn A   Flower centre 1g
Yarn B   Petals 2g
Yarn C   Base colour 5g

Any dk yarn will work for this pattern (Yarn quantities are based on average requirements for the yarn suggested and are therefore approximate measurements.)

Tension/gauge
Tension is not critical for this project, but it may affect the yarn quantities required.

Finished measurements
10cm X 10cm

THIS PATTERN IS WRITTEN WITH U.K. TERMS
(Key: U.K. terms)

Ch = chain
Sp = space
St = stitch
Ss = slip stitch
Dc = Double crochet
Tr = Treble crochet
... = repeat instructions
Beg = beginning

Changing yarn
You have to change the yarn colour frequently in this pattern. Please see page 82 for a detailed explanation of how to do this.

Coaster
Using yarn A, make a magic ring.
Round 1 ch3 (counts as first tr throughout), 11tr into ring, ss into top of beg ch3 to join, **fasten off.** (12tr)

Round 2 Using yarn B, join yarn into any st, ch3, 1tr into st at base of ch3, 1tr into next st, change to yarn C, 1tr into the same st, change to yarn B, *2tr into next st, 1tr into next st, change to yarn C, 1tr into the same st, change to yarn B; repeat from * until end ss in top beg ch3 to join. (24tr)

Round 3 ch3, 2tr into next st, 1tr into next st, change to yarn C, 2tr into next st, change to yarn B, *1tr into the next st, 2tr into next st, 1tr into the next st, change to yarn C, 2tr into next st, change to yarn B; repeat from * around until end, ss into top of beg ch3 to join. (36tr)

Round 4 ch1, 1dc into st at base of ch1, skip next st, then work 5tr in between stitches, skip next st, 1dc into the next st, change to yarn C, 1tr into next st, 2tr into next st, *change to yarn B, 1dc into next st, skip next st, then 5tr in between stitches, skip next st, 1dc into next st, change to yarn C, 1tr into next st, 2tr into next st; repeat from * until end, ss into beg dc to join. **Fasten off yarn B**, continue with yarn C.

At the end of round 4, your coaster should be looking like this.

Round 5 ch1, 1dc into st at base of ch1, 1dc into each st around, ss into beg dc to join. (60dc)

Round 6 ch1, 1dc into st at base of ch1, 1dc into next 2 sts, 2dc into next st, *1dc into next 9 sts, 2dc into next st; repeat from * 4 more times, then 1dc into next 6 sts, ss into beg dc to join, **fasten off**. (66dc)

Sew in your ends and you are done!

SKILL LEVEL

Bookmark

The first thing I ever crocheted was a flower just like this one. It's a great project to start with, simple and small, so you don't get overwhelmed.

You will need:
- 3mm hook (or corresponding hook to reach gauge)
- Dk yarn – approx 3g

Recommended yarn
Paintbox Yarns, Cotton, Dk
Yarn A Flower centre <1g
Yarn B Flower petals 1g
Yarn C Stem and leaf 1g

Any dk yarn will work for this pattern (Yarn quantities are based on average requirements for the yarn suggested and are therefore approximate measurements.)

Tension/gauge
Tension is not critical for this project, but it may affect the yarn quantities required.

Finished measurements
Flower 5cm, length 27cm

THIS PATTERN IS WRITTEN WITH U.K. TERMS
(Key: U.K. terms)

Ch = chain
Sp = space
St = stitch
Ss = slip stitch
Dc = double crochet
Tr = treble crochet
Htc = half treble crochet
Dtr = double treble crochet
... = repeat instructions
Beg = beginning

Flower

Using yarn A, make a magic ring.
Round 1 ch1, 12dc into ring, ss into beg dc to join, **fasten off**.

Round 2 Join yarn B into any st, *ch3, 2dtr into next st, ch3, ss into next st; repeat from * 5 more times, working last ss into the same st you joined, **fasten off**.

Now that you know how to make a basic crocheted flower, the possibilities are endless!

Stem

Join yarn C into the same stitch you started and finished the petals in. Ch50 (this will be the length of the boookmark, you can alter the amount of ch to create the desired length). **Do not fasten off**.

Adjust the length of your stem for different book sizes.

Place the 2 leaves up so they are sitting in a heart shape. Then turn the leaves over to the back, holding them in place. Use the tail end to sew back and forth a few times to hold it in place.

Leaf

Leaf 1 1dc into 2nd ch from hook, 1htr into next ch, 1tr into next ch, 1htr into next ch, 1dc into next ch, ss into next ch.

Leaf 2 ch6, 1dc into 2nd ch from hook, 1htr into next ch, 1tr into next ch, 1htr into next ch, 1dc into next ch, ss into same ch as leaf 1, **fasten off**.

Use the tail end to sew the leaves into a heart shape.

Sew in the ends and you are done!

Granny squares & stripes cardigan

SKILL LEVEL

This was one of my very first designs. You just can't go wrong with a granny square cardigan!

You will need:
- 5mm hook (or corresponding hook to reach gauge)
- Dk acrylic yarn
- Stitch marker
- Button (optional)

Recommended yarn
Stylecraft Special, dk, acrylic
- Magenta (base colour)
- Matador
- Jaffa
- Dandelion
- Kelly Green
- Cloud Blue
- French Navy
- Boysenberry
- Fondant
- Bright Pink

THIS PATTERN IS WRITTEN WITH U.K. TERMS
(Key: U.K. terms)

Ch = chain
Sp = space
St = stitch
Ss = slip stitch
Dc = double crochet
Htr = half treble crochet
Tr = treble crochet
Dtr = double treble crochet
Dc2tog = double crochet 2 together
... = repeat instructions
Beg = beginning

Tension/gauge

It is important to get your tension correct or it will effect the size of the garment. Make sure the size of your squares matches the measurement in the table for your size. Do a test square (up to round 4, using the instructions for your size) and change your hook size accordingly.

	XS	S	M	L	XL/2XL	3XL	4XL/5XL
Square (cm) after round 4, after blocking	9x9	10x10	11x11	12.5x12.5	14x14	11x11	12.5x12.5

Tension for sleeve

10cm X 10cm = 16 sts X 8 rows of granny stripe stitch (before blocking)

Sizing

This is a standard-fitting piece; keep this in mind when choosing which size to go for. To measure your bust/chest, measure around the fullest part of your bust.

	XS	S	M	L	XL/2XL	3XL	4XL/5XL
To fit chest/Bust (cm)	71-76	81-86	91.5-96.5	101.5-106.5	111.5-127	132-137	142-158
Circumference of finished garment (cm)	90	100	110	125	140	154	175

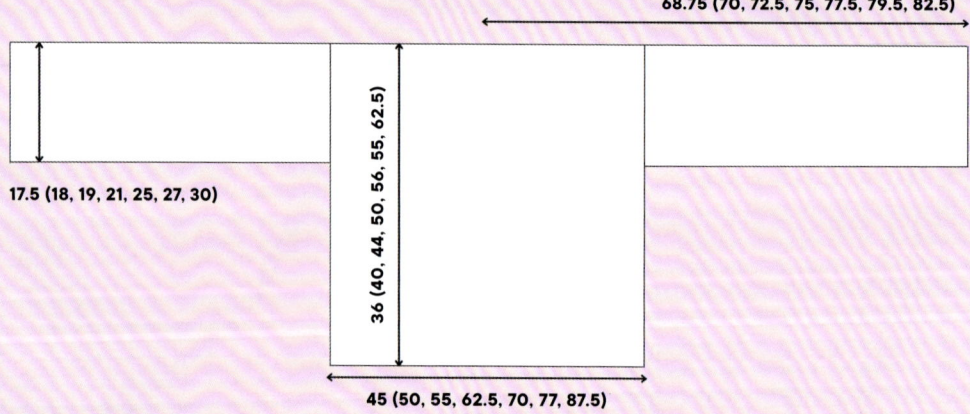

68.75 (70, 72.5, 75, 77.5, 79.5, 82.5)
17.5 (18, 19, 21, 25, 27, 30)
36 (40, 44, 50, 56, 55, 62.5)
45 (50, 55, 62.5, 70, 77, 87.5)

Yarn quantities

Quantities for each size are shown in the table. They are based on average requirements, when using the yarn suggested, and are therefore approximate measurements. Other yarns will work but it may effect the amount of yarn needed.

	XS	S	M	L	XL/2XL	3XL	4XL/5XL
Yarn A, base colour	145g/430m	150g/445m	155g/455m	200g/590m	220g/650m	275g/810m	295g/870m
Yarn B-J (amount of each colour)	30g/90m	35g/105m	35g/105m	35g/105m	45g/135m	55g/160m	60g/175m

Cardigan construction

The body of the cardigan is made with granny squares. The granny squares are attached together using the 'join as you go method' into the formation, for your size, shown in the diagram. You will then work the sleeves onto the body, working in the round.

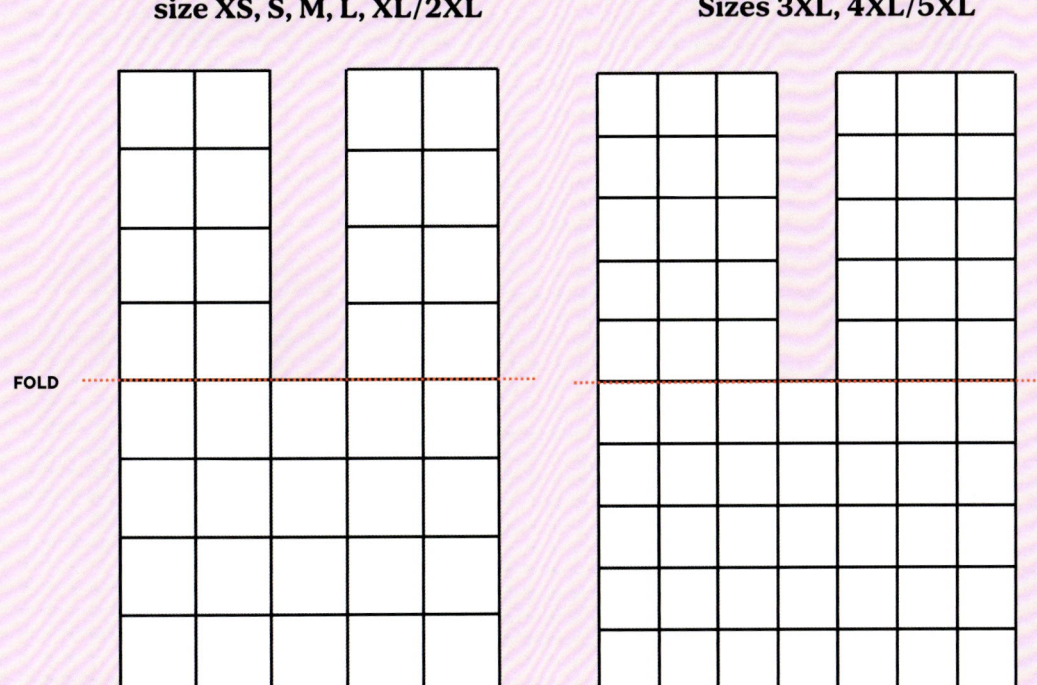

size XS, S, M, L, XL/2XL

Sizes 3XL, 4XL/5XL

FOLD

TIPS

- Sizes XS, S, M, L & XL/2XL make 4 of each square. Total = 36 squares
- Sizes 3XL & 4XL/5XL make 7 of each square, choose your favourite square and make 1 extra. Total = 64 squares

Granny square

Make all your squares up to round 3
XS, S, M, L & XL/2XL – 36 squares
3XL & 4XL/5XL – 64 squares

SIZE XS
ch4, ss into first ch to join and made a ring.
Round 1 ch2 (counts as first htr throughout), 2htr into ring, (ch2, 3htr) 3 times, ch2, ss into top of beg ch2 to join, **fasten off.**

Round 2 Join new yarn in ch2 sp, ch2, (2htr, ch2, 3htr) into same ch2 sp, ch1, * (3htr, ch2, 3htr) into next ch2 sp, ch1; repeat from * 2 more times, ss into top of beg ch2 to join, **fasten off.**

Round 3 Join new yarn into any ch2 sp, ch2, (2htr, ch2, 3htr) into same ch2 sp, ch1, 3htr in next ch1 sp, ch1 *(3htr, ch2, 3htr) into next ch2 sp, ch1, 3htr into next ch1 sp, ch1; repeat from * 2 more times, ss into top of beg ch2 to join, **fasten off.**

SIZES S, M, L, XL/2XL, 3XL & 4XL/5XL
Round 1 ch3 (counts as first tr throughout), 2tr into ring, (ch2, 3tr) 3 times, ch2, ss into top of beg ch3 to join, **fasten off.**

Round 2 Join new yarn in ch2 sp, ch3, (2tr, ch2, 3tr) into same ch2 sp, ch1, *(3tr, ch2, 3tr) into next ch2 sp, ch1; repeat from * 2 more times, ss into top of beg ch3 to join, **fasten off.**

SIZES S, M, L, 3XL & 4XL/5XL
Round 3 Join new yarn into any ch2 sp, ch3, (2tr, ch2, 3tr) into same ch2 sp, ch1, 3tr into next ch1 sp, ch1 *(3tr, ch2, 3tr) into next ch2 sp, ch1, 3tr into next ch1 sp, ch1; repeat from * 2 more times, ss into top of beg ch3 to join, **fasten off.**

Image shows granny square after round 3 for sizes S, M, L, 3XL & 4XL/5XL.

SIZE XL/2XL
Round 3 Join new yarn into any ch2 sp, ch4 (counts as first dtr), (2dtr, ch2, 3dtr) into same ch2 sp, ch1, 3dtr into next ch1 sp, ch1 *(3dtr, ch2, 3dtr) into next ch2 sp, ch1, 3dtr into next ch1 sp, ch1; repeat from * 2 more times, ss into top of beg ch2 to join, **fasten off.**

With round 4 you will use the 'join as you go' method to attach the squares into the formation shown in the diagram for your size. Round 4 for each size. The 'join as you go' instructions use a tr stitch, however if you need to use an htr or a dtr for your size, swap the tr for the stitch needed.

First square
SIZES XS & S
Round 4 (Join as you go) Join new yarn into any ch2 sp, ch2, (2htr, ch2, 3htr) into same ch2 sp, ch1, 3htr into next ch1 sp, ch1, 3htr into next ch1 sp, ch1 *(3htr, ch2, 3htr) into next ch2 sp, ch1, 3htr into next ch1 sp, ch1, 3htr into next ch1 sp, ch1; repeat from * 2 more times, ss into top of beg ch2 to join, **fasten off.**

SIZES M & 3XL
Round 4 (Join as you go) Join new yarn into any ch2 sp, ch3, (2tr, ch2, 3tr) into same ch2 sp, ch1, 3tr into next ch1 sp, ch1, 3tr in next ch1 sp, ch1 *(3tr, ch2, 3tr) into next ch2 sp, ch1, 3tr into next ch1 sp, ch1, 3tr into next ch1 sp, ch1; repeat from * 2 more times, ss into top of beg ch3 to join, **fasten off.**

SIZES L, XL/2XL & 4XL/5XL
Round 4 (Join as you go) Join new yarn into any ch2 sp, ch4 (counts as first dtr), (2dtr, ch2, 3dtr) into same ch2 sp, ch1, 3dtr into next ch1 sp, ch1, 3dtr into next ch1 sp, ch1 *(3dtr, ch2, 3dtr) into next ch2 sp, ch1, 3dtr into next ch1 sp, ch1, 3dtr into next ch1 sp, ch1; repeat from* 2 more times, ss into top of beg ch4 to join, **fasten off.**

Crochet your first square as the instructions explain. Then use the 'join as you go' method to attach your other squares.

Join as you go

1. Crochet your first square up to the round before the last round. (square 1)
2. With your next square (square 2) start the final round, leaving the corner unfinished. (Your corner should be 3tr, ch2, 3tr.) Stop after the first 3tr.
3. ch1, ss into the adjoining corner of 'square 1'. Finish corner as usual with 3tr.
4. ss into next ch1 space of 'square 1' *3tr as usual into 'square 2', ss into next ch1 space of 'square 1'; repeat as many times as needed until you are at the ch2 corner sp.
5. 3tr into the corner space of 'square 2', ss into the adjoining corner of 'square 1', ch1, finish corner as usual with 3tr.
6. Finish square as you normally would, **fasten off**.

Step 2

Step 4

Step 5

Step 6

Attaching on 2 sides

1. Repeat the same steps as before for one side.
2. When you get to the second corner of the square, 3tr as usual, then ss into the corner of the square above, then ss into the corner of the square to the left.
3. Finish the other side of the square, joining as you go like before.
4. Finish the square like you normally would, **fasten off**.

Step 1

Step 2

Step 4

Join your squares together so it looks something like this. Check the diagram on page 23 for your size square layout.

Fold the piece in half at the shoulder seams and place a stitch marker 40 (40, 38, 35, 29, 43, 39) sts up from the bottom hem.

This marks the armhole opening. Sew the side seams together using a mattress stitch, working from the bottom hem up to the stitch marker, matching the stitches.

TIP
- *Each square has 17 sts (each ch1 sp counts as a stitch).*

Granny stripe stitch

You will be using the granny stripe stitch for the sleeves. For this stitch you are working in between the stitches. Not into the top of the stitch like you might normally do. You are working stitches like you would with a granny square. Round 1 of the sleeve, you will be doing a standard tr st around working into the stitches, then with round 2 you will work inbetween stitches.

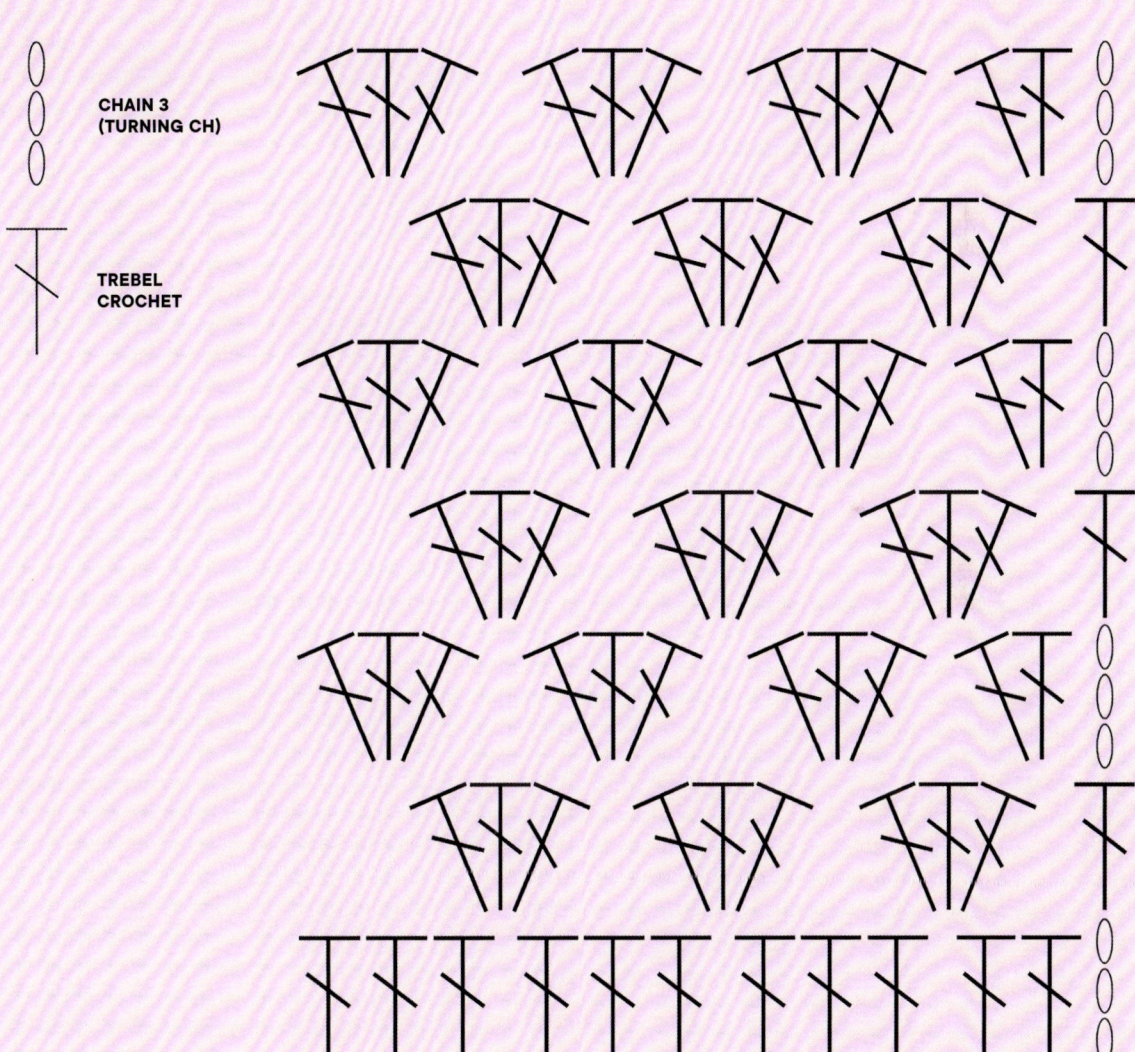

CHAIN 3 (TURNING CH)

TREBEL CROCHET

Sleeve

Join yarn A into any st of the sleeve opening (I suggest doing it by the side seam).

SIZES XS, S & 4XL/5XL

Round 1 ch3 (counts as first tr throughout), 1tr into st at base of ch3, then 1tr into each st around, ss into top of beg ch3 to join. (57, 57, 93 tr)

SIZES M, L, XL/2XL & 3XL

Round 1 ch3 (counts as first tr throughout), 1tr into each st around, ss into top of beg ch3 to join. (60, 66, 78, 84 tr)

ALL SIZES

Round 2 ch3 and turn, 2tr in between 2 sts at the base of ch3, skip 3 sts, *3tr in between sts, skip 3 sts; repeat from * around, ss into top of beg ch3. Repeat round 2 until 37 (36, 36, 35, 34, 33, 31) rounds have been worked, then move onto the cuff.

This table shows how many rows of each colour to do for each size. When changing colours you want to fasten off and join the new yarn between any 3tr group.

Round 2 of sleeve

	XS	S	M	L	XL/2XL	3XL	4XL/5XL
Magenta	3	2	2	2	1	1	1
Matador	3	3	3	3	3	3	3
Jaffa	3	3	3	3	3	3	3
Dandelion	3	3	3	3	3	3	3
Magenta	2	2	2	2	2	2	1
Kelly Green	3	3	3	3	3	3	3
Cloud Blue	3	3	3	3	3	3	3
French Navy	3	3	3	3	3	3	3
Magenta	2	2	2	2	2	2	1
Boysenberry	3	3	3	3	3	3	3
Fondant	3	3	3	3	3	3	3
Bright Pink	3	3	3	3	3	3	3
Magenta	3	3	3	2	2	1	1

Cuff
TIP
- Turn if needed so you are working right side facing front.

SIZES XS, S & 4XL/5XL
Round 1 ch1, 1dc into the first st, then dc2tog around, ss into beg dc to join. (29, 29, 47 dc)

SIZES M, L, XL/2XL & 3XL
Round 1 ch1, dc2tog around, ss into beg dc to join. (30, 33, 39, 42 dc)

ALL SIZES
Round 2 ch1, 1dc into each st around, ss into beg dc to join, **fasten off**. (29, 29, 30, 33, 39, 42, 47 dc)

Repeat sleeve and cuff on the opposite side for the 2nd sleeve.

Hem
TIP
- You will be working around the whole inside body of the cardigan and the bottom hem.

Join yarn into ch2 corner sp of cardigan hem/opening (shown on diagram with *).

TIP
- Each square has 17 sts (each ch1 sp counts as a stitch).

Round 1 ch1, 4dc into ch2 sp, 1dc into each st until next ch2 sp, 4dc into ch2 sp, 1dc into each st until end, ss into beg dc to join, **fasten off**.

Add a button (optional)
Sew a button onto one side of the cardigan opening and use the ch sp from the granny square on the opposite side for a button hole.

Sew in your ends and you are done!

If you are left-handed, you will need to join into the opposite corner.

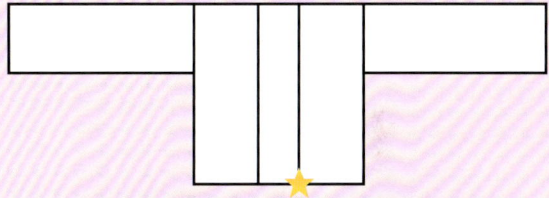

SKILL LEVEL

Raglan short-sleeved jumper

A basic raglan jumper, but with shorter sleeves so it works up faster. Have fun with the colours of this one to make it your own.

You will need:

- 6mm hook - used for body (or corresponding hook to reach gauge)
- 5mm hook - used for ribbing (or 1 hook size smaller than what was needed to reach gauge)
- Aran yarn

Recommended yarn

Drops Air, aran, wool mix

Yarn A — Moss Green
Yarn B — Pink
Yarn C — Crimson Red
Yarn D — Pistachio Ice Cream
Yarn E — Electric Orange
Yarn F — Lemonade
Yarn G — Light Blue
Yarn H — Off White Uni

Tension/gauge

Before blocking - 10cm X 10cm = 12 sts X 7 Rows (of treble crochet stitch)
Change your hook size accordingly

THIS PATTERN IS WRITTEN WITH U.K. TERMS
(Key: U.K. terms)

Ch = chain
Sp = space
St = stitch
Ss = slip stitch
Dc = double crochet
Tr = treble crochet
... = repeat instructions
Beg = beginning

Sizing

This is a standard fitting piece; keep this in mind when choosing the size best for you. The jumper has short sleeves and is lightly cropped. You can easily make the jumper longer and the sleeves longer but this will affect the amount of yarn needed. (Measurements before blocking)

	XS	S	M	L	XL	2XL	3XL	4XL	5XL
To fit chest/Bust (cm)	71-76	81-86	91.5-96.5	101.5-106.5	111.5-117	122-127	132-137	142-147	152-158
Finished circumference (cm)	93	100	107	113	127	140	147	160	167
Finished length (cm)	43	45	46.5	48	51.5	55	56.5	60	61.5
Sleeve circumference (cm)	37	40	43	47	53	60	63	70	73

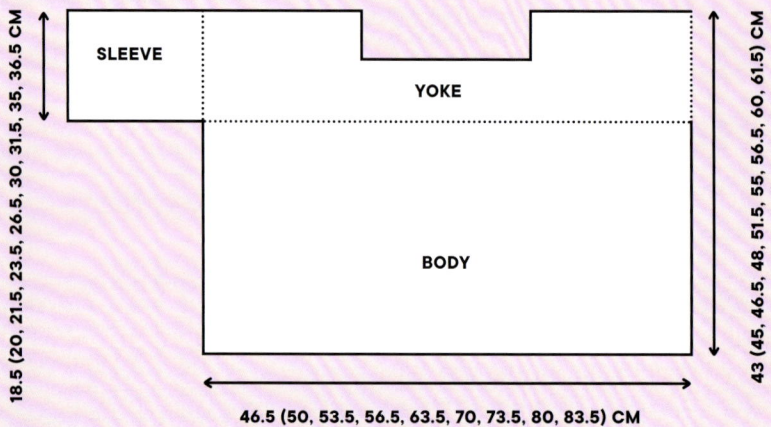

Yarn quantities

Quantities for each size are shown in the table. They are based on average requirements when using Drops Air yarn and are therefore approximate measurements. Other yarns will work but it may affect the amount of yarn needed. Yarn quantities are based off using 7 colours in the body, changing yarn colour every round.

	XS	S	M	L	XL	2XL	3XL	4XL	5XL
Total base (Yarn A-G)	210g/630m	245g/735m	245g/735m	245g/735m	280g/840m	315g/945m	350g/1050m	385g/1155m	385g/1155m
Total ribbing (Yarn H)	40g/120m	40g/120m	45g/135m	45g/135m	45g/135m	50g/150m	55g/165m	60g/180m	60g/180m
Amount of each (Yarn A-G)	30g/90m	35g/105m	35g/105m	35g/105m	40g/120m	45g/135m	50g/150m	55g/165m	55g/165m

Jumper construction

The jumper is worked from the top down. You will increase by working rounds into the yoke. The yoke is then folded and the 2 short sizes become arm holes. You will then work the rest of the body in the round and add length to the sleeves. The hem, neck and arm cuffs are added at the end. The way the pattern is written means, for the yoke, **you always start and end in the ch2 corner space**. This helps to make a less visible joining seam.

Yoke

It is up to you when you change yarn colour (if you do at all) so changing yarn won't be included in the instructions.

Using yarn A, ch72 (72, 72, 72, 72, 88, 88, 88, 88), then ss into beg ch to join and make a loop (make sure your ch isn't twisted).

Round 1 ch3 (counts as first tr throughout), 1tr into each ch, ss into top of beg ch3 to join. (72, 72, 72, 72, 72, 88, 88, 88, 88 tr)

Round 2 ch3 and turn, 1tr into same st as ch3, 1tr into next 22 (22, 22, 22, 22, 26, 26, 26, 26) sts, 2tr into next st, ch2, 2tr into next st, 1tr into next 10 (10, 10, 10, 10, 14, 14, 14, 14) sts, 2tr into next st, ch2, 2tr into next st, 1tr into next 22 (22, 22, 22, 22, 26, 26, 26, 26) sts, 2tr into next st, ch2, 2tr into next st, 1tr into next 10 (10, 10, 10, 10, 14, 14, 14, 14) sts, 2tr into next st, ch2, ss into top of beg ch3 to join. (80, 80, 80, 80, 80, 96, 96, 96, 96 tr + 8ch)

Round 3

Round 3 ch3 and turn, 1tr into ch2 sp, 1tr into each st until ch2 sp, *(2tr, ch2, 2tr) into ch2 sp, 1tr into each st until next ch2 sp; Repeat from * 2 more times, then 2tr into ch2 sp, ch2, ss into beg ch3 to join. Repeat round 3 until 7 (8, 9, 10, 12, 13, 14, 16, 17) rounds have been worked.

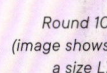

Round 10 (image shows a size L)

YOKE STITCH COUNT

Round 3 - (96, 96, 96, 96, 96, 112, 112, 112, 112 tr + 8ch)
Round 4 - (112, 112, 112, 112, 112, 128, 128, 128, 128 tr + 8ch)
Round 5 - (128, 128, 128, 128, 128, 144, 144, 144, 144 tr + 8ch)
Round 6 - (144, 144, 144, 144, 144, 160, 160, 160, 160 tr + 8ch)
Round 7 - (160, 160, 160, 160, 160, 176, 176, 176, 176 tr + 8ch)
Round 8 - (176, 176, 176, 176, 192, 192, 192, 192 tr + 8ch)
Round 9 - (192, 192, 192, 208, 208, 208, 208 tr + 8ch)
Round 10 - (208, 208, 224, 224, 224, 224 tr + 8ch)
Round 11 - (224, 240, 240, 240, 240 tr + 8ch)
Round 12 - (240, 256, 256, 256, 256 tr + 8ch)
Round 13 - (272, 272, 272, 272 tr + 8ch)
Round 14 - (288, 288, 288 tr + 8ch)
Round 15 - (304, 304 tr + 8ch)
Round 16 - (320, 320 tr + 8ch)
Round 17 - (336 tr + 8ch)

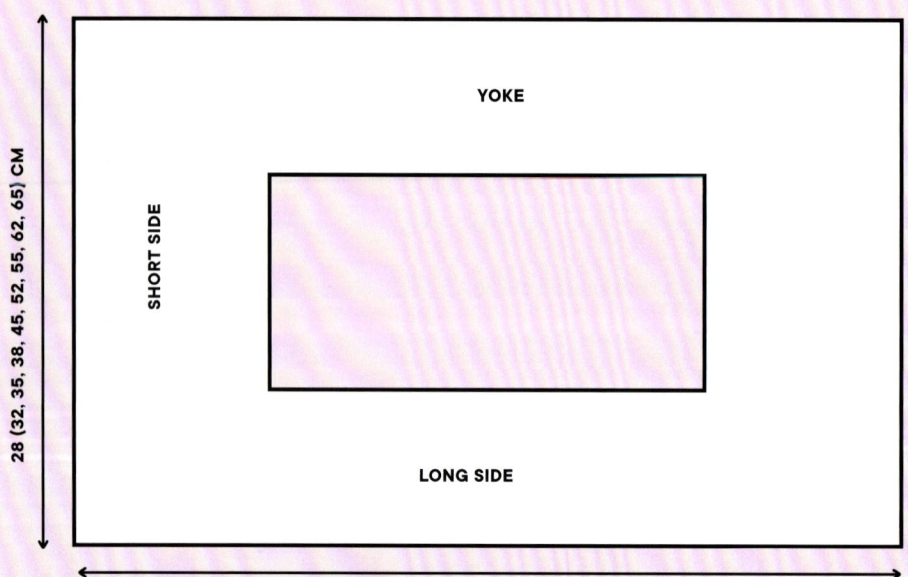

When you have completed the amount of rounds needed for your size your yoke should be the measurements shown in the diagram. If they are not; do more or less rounds so the measurements do match up. Alternately, try on the yoke; it should sit slightly off your shoulders.

Body

The long sides from the front and back of the body, The short sides form each sleeve. Because you are turning each round you may be about to work the 'long' side of your yoke first or the 'short' side first; follow the correct instructions for you.

TIP
- Simply; you will now be skipping the 'short' side of your yoke and only working into the stitches along the 'long' side. You will be working 2tr into each ch2 corner sp, and chaining 6 instead of working the 'short' side. This is to create the arm holes.

WORKING 'SHORT' SIDE FIRST

Round 1 ch3 and turn, 1tr into same ch2 sp, ch6, skip the whole 'short' side of the yoke, 2tr into next ch2 sp, 1tr into each st along 'long' side until next ch2 sp, 2tr into ch2 sp, ch6, skip the whole 'short' side of the yoke, 2tr into next ch2 sp, 1tr into each st of 'long' side until next ch2 sp, ss into top of beg ch3 to join. (100, 108, 116, 124, 140, 156, 164, 180, 188 tr + ch12)

WORKING 'LONG' SIDE FIRST

Round 1 ch3 and turn, 1tr into each st of 'long' side until next ch2 sp, 2tr into ch2 sp, ch6, skip the whole 'short' side of the yoke, 2tr into next ch2 sp, 1tr into each st of 'long' side until next ch2 sp, 2tr into ch2 sp, ch6, skip the whole 'short' side of the yoke, 1tr into same ch2 sp as beg ch3, ss into top of beg ch3 to join. (100, 108, 116, 124, 140, 156, 164, 180, 188 tr + ch12)

TIP
- For round 2 - Each tr st and ch count as a st.

Round 2-17 ch3 and turn, 1tr into each st until end, ss into top of beg ch3 to join. After round 17 change to yarn G. (112, 120, 128, 136, 152, 168, 176, 192, 200 tr)

TIP
- If you would like your jumper to be longer, do more rounds until you are happy with the length. Keep in mind you will be adding 5cm of ribbing.

After round 1, you will have created the arm hole and will now be working on the body.

The yoke and body are now complete. Move on to the ribbing and sleeves.

Row 1 (before ss into round 1)

Row 1

Row 2

Row 4 (before ss into round 1).

Hem ribbing

Change to a 5mm hook (or 1 hook size smaller than hook used to reach gauge). Turn your work, if necessary, so your work is right side facing the front.

Round 1 ch1 (doesn't count as first dc st), 1dc into each st around, ss in to beg dc to join.

RIBBING
The ribbing is worked in rows off Round 1.

Row 1 ch11, 1dc into 2nd ch from hook, 1dc into each ch, ss into next 2 sts from round 1. (10dc 2ss)

Row 2 Turn your work, then skip 2 ss, 1dc into backloop only of each dc st. (10dc)

Row 3 ch1 and turn (doesn't count as first st), 1dc into backloop only of each dc st, ss into next 2 sts from round 1. (10dc + 2ss)

Repeat rows 2–3 until all sts from round 1 have been worked into.

Fasten off and sew the ends of the ribbing together.

Sleeve
TIP
- *If you would like a tighter fitting sleeve, change to a 5mm hook (or 1 hook size smaller than hook used to hit gauge).*

Join yarn into 1st ch at the bottom of the arm hole opening.

Round 1 ch3 (counts as first tr st), 1tr into next 5 ch, 1tr around the post of tr st, 1tr into ch2 sp, 1tr into each st until next ch2 sp, 1tr into ch2 sp, 1tr around the post of tr st, ss into top of beg ch3 to join. (44, 48, 52, 56, 64, 72, 76, 84, 88 tr)

Rounds 2–6 ch3 and turn, 1tr into each st around, ss into top of beg ch-3 to join. Change to yarn H after round 6.

Round 1

Sleeve ribbing
Change to a 5mm hook (or 1 hook size smaller than hook used to reach gauge). Turn your work, if necessary, so your work is right side facing the front.

Round 1 ch1 (doesn't count as first dc st), 1dc into each st around, ss in to beg dc to join.

RIBBED STITCH - JOIN AS YOU GO
ch7, 1dc into 2nd ch from hook, 1dc into each ch. (6dc)

Repeat the same steps as 'hem ribbing'.

Repeat on the other side for the second sleeve.

Neck ribbing

Change to a 5mm hook (or 1 hook size smaller than hook used to reach gauge). Turn your work, if necessary, so your work is right side facing the front.

Join yarn H into any st around the next opening (I recommend joining around the shoulder so the seam is less visible).

Round 1 ch1 (doesn't count as first dc st), 1dc into each st around, ss in to beg dc to join.

RIBBED STITCH - JOIN AS YOU GO
ch7, 1dc into 2nd ch from hook, 1dc into each ch. (6dc)

Repeat the same steps as 'hem ribbing'.

Sew in your ends and you are all done!

These patterns are pieces you actually want to wear. A crocheted collar to change up a look, a chic granny square vest, a scrunchie to hold your hair back and the perfect everyday bag.

Out and about in the city

SKILL BUILDER

Essential crochet stiches

These are the stitches you need to know to be able to create the crochet patterns in this book. Once you have the basics, you should be able to make pretty much anything!

Slip knot
This is used to attach your yarn to your hook. Create a loop with your yarn and insert your hook into the loop, pull through the working end of the yarn. Pull the tail end of the yarn to tighten the loop onto your hook.

Chain (ch)
Wrap the yarn around your hook and pull through the loop on your hook.

Slip stitch (ss)
A ss is often used to join a round or to move the hook/yarn to a new point. To make a ss, insert your hook into your work, yarn over and pull through the work and the loop on your hook.

Double crochet (dc)
Insert your hook into your work, yarn over and pull through the work, you will then have 2 loops on your hook. Yarn over and pull through 2 loops.

SKILL BUILDER

Half treble crochet (htr)
Wrap the yarn around your hook, insert your hook into your work, yarn over and pull through the work, you will then have 3 loops on your hook. Yarn over and pull through all 3 loops.

Double treble crochet (dtr)
Wrap the yarn around your hook twice, insert your hook into your work, yarn over and pull through the work, you will then have 4 loops on your hook. *Yarn over and pull through 2 loops* 3 times.

Treble crochet (tr)
Wrap the yarn around your hook, insert your hook into your work, yarn over and pull through the work, you will then have 3 loops on your hook. *Yarn over and pull through 2 loops* twice.

Double crochet 2 together (dc2tog)
Insert your hook into your work, yarn over and pull through the work. Insert your hook into the next stitch, yarn over and pull through the work, you will then have 3 loops on your hook. Yarn over and pull through 3 loops.

Front post treble crochet (fptr)

Wrap the yarn around your hook, insert your hook behind the treble stitch post (from front to back, then back to front, so the post is in front of the hook). Yarn over and pull up a loop around the post of the stitch, *yarn over, pull through two loops* twice.

Treble crochet 2 together (tr2tog)

Wrap the yarn around your hook, insert your hook into your work, yarn over and pull through the work. You will then have 3 loops on your hook. Yarn over and pull through 2 loops. Wrap the yarn around your hook, insert your hook into the next stitch, yarn over and pull through the work. You will then have 4 loops on your hook. Yarn over and pull through 2 loops. Yarn over and pull through all 3 loops.

Granny stripe collar

SKILL LEVEL

The perfect accessory to personalise any outfit. Go for all different colours to make it pop, or one solid colour so it goes with everything.

You will need:
- 6mm hook (or corresponding hook to reach gauge)
- Aran yarn – approx 100g

Recommended yarn
OPTION 1: MULTICOLOURED STRIPE

Yarn A	Paintbox aran acrylic – Midnight Blue 30g
Yarn B	Paintbox aran acrylic – Blush Pink 15g
Yarn C	Paintbox aran acrylic – Washed Teal 6g
Yarn D	Stylecraft special aran acrylic – Bluebell 7g
Yarn E	Paintbox aran acrylic – Blood Orange 7g
Yarn F	Paintbox aran acrylic – Tea Rose 8g
Yarn G	Stylecraft special aran acrylic – Pistachio 8g
Yarn H	Paintbox aran acrylic – Lipstick Pink 9g
Yarn I	Paintbox aran acrylic – Mustard Yellow 10g

OPTION 2: WHITE
Yarn and Colors Epic cotton - White approx 100g

Any aran yarn will work for this project (Yarn quantities are based on average requirements for the yarn suggested and are therefore approximate measurements.)

Tension/gauge
Using the granny stripe stitch.
12 sts and 7 rows measure 10 X 10cm over granny stitch using a 6mm hook, or size needed to obtain correct tension.

Finished measurements
Neck hole approx 52cm, length of collar approx 15cm

THIS PATTERN IS WRITTEN WITH U.K. TERMS
(Key: U.K. terms)

Ch = chain
Sp = space
St = stitch
Ss = slip stitch
Dc = double crochet
Tr = treble crochet
... = repeat instructions
Beg = beginning

Granny stripe collar

Using yarn A, ch62

Row 1 1tr into 4th ch from hook, 1tr into each ch, change to yarn B, **fasten off yarn A**. (60tr)

Row 2 ch3 (counts as first tr throughout) and turn your work, 1tr into the next 3 sts, 2tr into next st, *1tr into the next 4 sts, 2tr into next st, repeat from * until end, change to yarn C, **fasten off yarn B**. (72tr)

Round 2. Keep working into the stitch like Round 1.

TIP
- For row 3, you are working in between sts, like you would for a granny square. You are making groups of sts. Have a look at the pictures.

Row 3 ch3 and turn, skip st, 2tr in between sts, skip 2 sts, 2tr in between sts, skip 2 sts, 3tr in between sts, *skip 2 sts, 2tr in between sts, skip 2 sts, 2tr in between sts, skip 2 sts, 3tr in between sts; repeat from *9 more times, then skip 2 sts, 2tr in between sts, skip 2 sts, 2tr in between sts, 1tr into the top of last st, change to yarn D, **fasten off yarn C**. (83tr)

For rounds 3–10 you will be working into the space in between the stitches.

Row 4 ch3 and turn, skip 2 sts, work 2tr in between groups of sts, *3tr in between next group of sts, 2tr in between next group of sts; repeat from * 15 more times, 3tr in between next group of sts then 1tr into the top of last st, change to yarn E, **fasten off yarn D**. (87tr)

Row 5 ch3 and turn, skip 3 sts, 3tr inbetween each group of sts till end, 1tr into the top of the last st, change to yarn F, **fasten off yarn E**. (101tr)

Row 6 ch3 and turn, skip 3 sts then work *3tr in between group of sts, 3tr in between next group of sts, 4tr in between next group of sts; repeat from * 9 more times, then 3tr in between next group of sts, 3tr in between next group of sts, 1tr into the top of the last st, change to yarn G, **fasten off yarn F**. (108tr)

Row 7 ch3 and turn, skip 3 sts then work *3tr in between group of sts, 4tr in between the next group of sts; repeat from * 14 more times, 3tr in between the next group of sts, 1tr into the top of the last st, change to yarn H, **fasten off yarn G**. (110tr)

Row 8 ch3 and turn, skip 3 sts then work, 4tr in between each group of sts until end, 1tr into the top of last st, change to yarn I, **fasten off yarn H**. (122tr)

Row 9 ch3 and turn, skip 4 sts then work, *4tr in between group of sts, 4tr in between the next group of sts, 5tr in between the next group of sts, repeat from * 8 more times, then 4tr in between the next group of sts, 4tr in between next group of sts, 1tr into the top of the last st, change to yarn B, **fasten off yarn I**. (127tr)

Row 10 ch3 and turn, skip 4 sts then work, *4tr in between group of sts, 5tr in between the next group of sts, repeat from * 13 more times, 1tr into the top of the last st, **fasten off**. (128tr)

Row 4

Row 10

Join in the first ch.

Working around the post of each tr st, work 2dc.

Round 1 of edging.

Round 2 of edging.

Fastening

Edging

Using yarn A join into the first ch.

Row 1 ch1, 2dc into the side of each tr st, (20dc) then work 1dc into each st along the bottom edge until you reach the other side (128dc), then 2dc into the side of each tr st along the other side (20dc). (Total 168dc).

Row 2 ch1 and turn, skip st at base of ch1, *skip 1 st, work 5tr into next st, skip 1 st, ss into next st; repeat from * until end, **fasten off**.

Fastening

Join yarn A into the top corner of the collar ch30, **fasten off**. Repeat for the other side.

Sew in any ends and you are done!

SKILL LEVEL

Grandad's vest

If you love granny squares like me, this is the pattern for you! Pair with your favourite jeans and some chunky jewellery for that grandad chic look.

You will need:
- 5mm hook (or corresponding hook to reach gauge)
- Aran, cotton yarn

Recommended yarn
Yarn and Colors Epic cotton yarn

Yarn A	Cotton Candy
Yarn B	Lime
Yarn C	Amazon
Yarn D	Denim
Yarn E	Ice Blue
Yarn F	Dark Blue
Yarn G	Orchid
Yarn H	Marble

> **THIS PATTERN IS WRITTEN WITH U.K. TERMS**
> *(Key: U.K. terms)*
> Ch = chain
> Sp = space
> St = stitch
> Ss = slip stitch
> Dc = double crochet
> Tr = treble crochet
> *...* = repeat instructions
> Beg = beginning

Tension/gauge

The body of the vest is made from granny squares. It is important to get the size of the squares correct so the size of the vest is. Change your hook size accordingly.

Granny square after round 4 = 13cm X 13cm (before blocking)

Sizing

This is a tight-fitting piece; keep this in mind when choosing which size to go for. If you want something more oversized go up a size or two. To measure your bust/chest, measure around the fullest part of your bust.

	XS	S-L	XL-2XL	3XL-5XL
To fit chest/Bust (cm)	71-76	81-106.5	111.5-127	132-158
Finished circumference of garment, after blocking (cm)	80	110	135	160
Finished length, after blocking (cm)	55	55	60	70

Yarn quantities

Quantities for each size are shown in the table. They are based on average requirements when using Yarn and Colors Epic cotton yarn and are therefore approximate measurements. Other yarns will work but it may effect the amount of yarn needed.

Choose the number of colours you want for the granny squares (up to round 3). Divide the total amount needed by the number of colours used to find out how much you will need of each colour. eg If you are making a size M/L and using 7 colours - 200g divided by 7 = around 29g of each colour.

	XS	S-L	XL-2XL	3XL-5XL
Total yarn used	335g/505m	415g/625m	690g/1035m	845g/1270m
Total yarn used for squares (up to round 3)	160g/240m	200g/300m	340g/510m	420g/630m
Base colour (yarn H)	110g/165m	140g/210m	240g/360m	295g/445m
Ribbing (yarn G)	65g/100m	75g/115m	110g/165m	130g/195m

Vest construction

Attach your squares in the formation shown in the diagram for your size. Suggested construction- attach all your squares for the body first, then attach the half squares/squares for the straps, then attach the triangles. The red dotted lines are fold lines and for each size, join the purple line with the purple line and the blue line with the blue line.

For this pattern make the squares, half squares and triangles you need for your size, up to round 3. With round 4 join as you go into the formation shown in the diagram for your size. Alternatively, you can crochet all the squares up to round 4 and then sew them together or use your favourite method to attach granny squares.

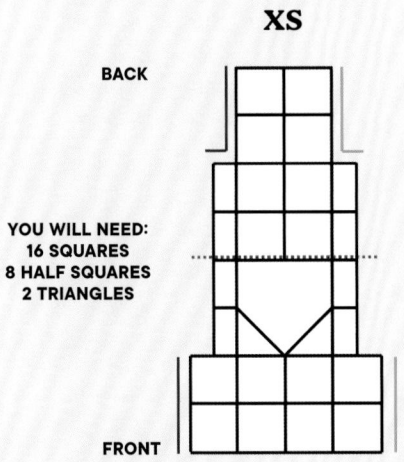

XS

BACK

YOU WILL NEED:
16 SQUARES
8 HALF SQUARES
2 TRIANGLES

FRONT

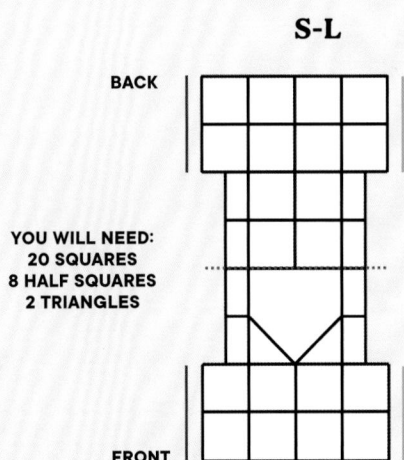

S-L

BACK

YOU WILL NEED:
20 SQUARES
8 HALF SQUARES
2 TRIANGLES

FRONT

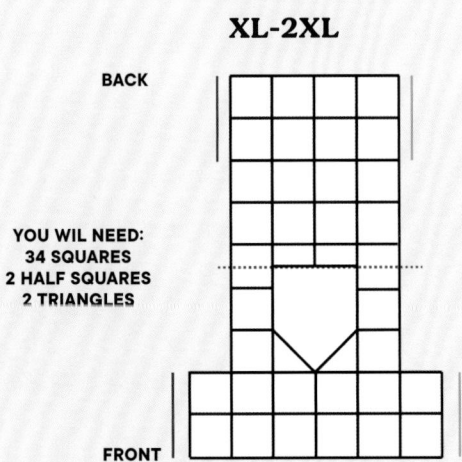

XL-2XL

BACK

YOU WIL NEED:
34 SQUARES
2 HALF SQUARES
2 TRIANGLES

FRONT

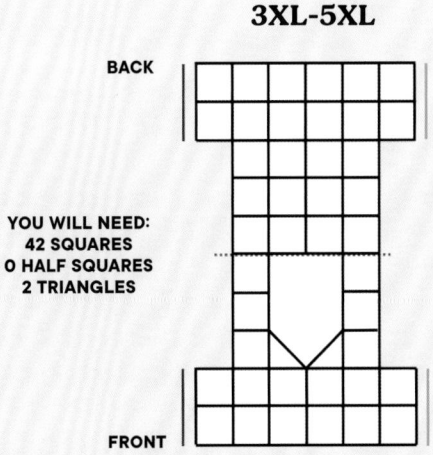

3XL-5XL

BACK

YOU WILL NEED:
42 SQUARES
0 HALF SQUARES
2 TRIANGLES

FRONT

Granny squares

Ch4, ss to first ch to join and made a ring.

Round 1 ch3 (counts as first tr throughout), 2tr into ring, (ch2, 3tr) 3 times, ch2, ss into top of beg ch3 to join. **Fasten off.**

Round 2 Join new colour into ch2 sp, ch3, (2tr, ch2, 3tr) into same ch2 sp, ch1, *(3tr, ch2, 3tr) into next ch2 sp, ch1; repeat from * 2 more times, ss into top of beg ch3 to join. **Fasten off.**

Round 3 Join new colour into any ch2 sp, ch3, (2tr, ch2, 3tr) into same ch2 sp, ch1, 3tr into next ch1 sp, ch1 *(3tr, ch2, 3tr) into next ch2 sp, ch1, 3tr in next ch1 sp, ch1; repeat from * 2 more times, ss into top of beg ch3 to join. **Fasten off.**

Round 4 (Join as you go) Join new yarn into any ch2 sp, ch3, (2tr, ch2, 3tr) into same ch2 sp, ch1, 3tr into next ch1 sp, ch1, 3tr into next ch1 sp, ch1 *(3tr, ch2, 3tr) into next ch2 sp, (ch1, 3tr) into each ch1 sp, ch1; repeat from* 2 more times, ss into top of beg ch3 to join. **Fasten off.**

Round 4. Create your first square up to round 4, then use the join as you go method to attach the other squares.

Step 2

Join as you go

1. Crochet your first square to the end of round 4. (square 1).
2. With your next square (square 2), work to end of round 3. Start next round with a (ch3, 2tr) in corner for the first 3 stitches.
3. ch1, ss into the adjoining corner of 'square 1'. Finish corner as usual with 3tr.

Step 4

4　ss into next ch1 space of 'square 1' *3tr as usual into 'square 2', ss into next ch1 space of 'square 1'; repeat as many times as needed until you are at the ch2 corner sp.
5　3tr into the corner space of 'square 2', ss into the adjoining corner of 'square 1', ch1, finish corner as usual with 3tr.
6　Finish square as you normally would, **fasten off**.

Attaching on 2 sides
1　Repeat the same steps as before for one side.
2　When you get to the second corner of the square, 3tr as usual, then ss into the corner of the square above, then ss into the corner of the square to the left.
3　Finish the other side of the square, joining as you go like before.
4　Finish the square like you normally would, **fasten off**.

Step 5

Step 6

Step 1

Step 2

Step 4

Half granny square

Ch4, ss into first ch to join and made a ring.

Round 1 ch3 (counts as first tr throughout), 3tr into ring, (ch2, 3tr) into ring twice, 1tr into ring, **fasten off**.

Round 2 (Working right side facing front throughout) join new yarn into top of ch3 from previous round, ch4, (counts as 1tr + ch1 throughout), *(3tr, ch2, 3tr, ch1) into each ch2 sp, 1tr into top of last tr st from previous round, **fasten off**.

Round 3 Join new yarn into 3rd ch of ch4 from previous round, ch3, 3tr into ch1 sp at base of ch3, ch1, (3tr, ch2, 3tr) into ch2 sp, ch1, 3tr into ch1 sp, ch1, (3tr, ch2, 3tr) into ch2 sp, ch1, 3tr into ch1 sp, 1tr into top of last tr of previous round, **fasten off**.

Round 4 (Join as you go) join new yarn into top of ch3 from previous round, ch4, (3tr, ch1) into next ch1 sp, (3tr, ch2, 3tr) into ch2 sp, ch1, (3tr, ch1) into each ch1 sp, (3tr, ch2, 3tr) into ch2 sp, ch1, (3tr, ch1) into next ch1 sp, 1tr into top of last tr of previous round, **fasten off**.

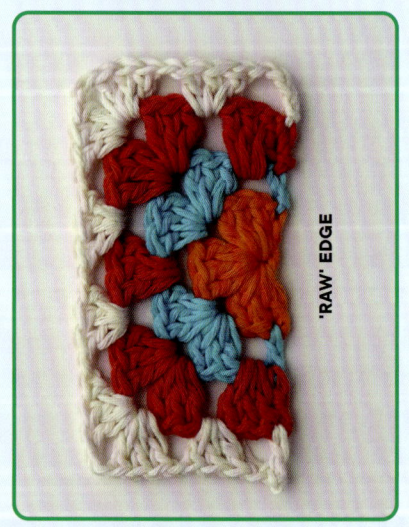

The 'raw edge' is important when joining to the vest. The 'raw edge' will be by the arm hole.

Square - join as you go - half square

1. Crochet your half square up to round 3.
2. Join yarn into top of ch3 from previous round, ch2, ss into middle ch1 sp of the square you are joining to. (If you are joining to the top of another half square - ss into the top of the adjacent tr st of the square you are joining to).
3. 3tr into next ch1 sp.
4. ss into next ch1 sp of the square you are joining to.
5. 3tr into ch2 sp, ss into ch2 corner sp of the square you are joining to, ch1.
6. Finish square as you normally would or continue to join as you go as you normally would.

The 'raw' edge of the half-granny square goes around the armhole.

Joining the square on the other side

1. Crochet your half square up to round 3.
2. Round 4 (you may need to join as you go like you would with a normal square on one side) when you get to the 2nd corner - 3tr, ch1 then ss into ch2 corner sp of the square you are joining to.
3. 3tr into same ch2 sp you just worked 3tr.
4. ss into next ch1 sp of the square you are joining to.
5. 3tr into next ch1 sp.
6. ss into the middle ch1 space of the square you are attaching to or if you are joining to another half square, ss into 3rd of 4ch of the square you are joining to.
7. ch3, ss into last st of previous round, **fasten off**.

Granny triangle

Ch4, ss into first ch to join and made a ring.

Round 1 ch4 (counts as first tr + ch1 throughout), 3tr into ring, (ch2, 3tr) into ring, ch1, 1tr into ring, **fasten off.**

Round 2 (Work right side facing throughout) join new yarn into 3rd ch of ch4 from previous round, ch4, 3tr into ch1 sp (space at base of ch4), ch1, (3tr, ch2, 3tr) into ch2 sp, ch1, 3tr into ch1 sp, ch1, 1tr into last tr st from previous round, **fasten off.**

Round 3 Join new yarn into 3rd ch of ch4 from previous round, ch4, 3tr into ch1 sp at base of ch4, ch1, 3tr into next ch1 sp, ch1, (3tr, ch2, 3tr) into ch2 sp, ch1, 3tr into next ch1 sp, ch1, 3tr into next ch1 sp, ch1, 1tr into last tr st from previous round, **fasten off.**

Round 4 (Join as you go) join new yarn into 3rd ch of ch4 from previous round, ch3, 3tr into ch1 sp at base of ch3, ch1, (3tr, ch1) into each ch1 sp, (3tr, ch2, 3tr) into ch2 sp, ch1, (3tr, ch1) into each ch1 sp, 1tr into last tr st from previous round, **fasten off.**

'RAW' EDGE

Triangle - join as you go

1. Crochet your triangle up to round 3.
2. Join yarn into 3rd ch of ch4 from previous round, ch2, ss into corner ch2 sp of the square you are joining to.
3. 3tr into ch1 sp at base of ch3.
4. ss into next ch1 sp of the square you are joining to.
5. *3tr into next ch1 sp, ss into next ch1 sp of the square you are joining to; Repeat from * once more.
6. 3tr into ch2 sp, ss into ch2 corner sp of the square to the right and ss into ch2 corner sp of the square above you are joining to.
7. 3tr into same sp you just did 3tr.
8. ss into next ch1 sp of the square you are joining to, 3tr into next ch1 sp; Repeat 2 more times.
9. ss into the ch2 sp of the square you are joining to.
10. ch3, ss into last st of previous round, **fasten off.**

The 'raw' edge of the triangle creates the neckline.

Front

Back

Arm hole ribbing

Join yarn into any st around the arm hole. (I like to do it by the side seam so it is less visible).

Round 1 ch1 (doesn't count as first st), 1dc into each st around (2dc into the side of each tr st), ss into beg dc to join.

TIP
- The 'raw' edge of a half square has 16 sts.

Ribbing
The ribbing is worked in rows off round 1.

Row 1 ch5, 1dc into 2nd ch from hook, 1dc into each ch, ss into next 2 sts from round 1. (4dc + 2ss)
Row 2 Turn your work, then skip 2 ss, 1dc into backloop only of each dc st. (4dc)
Row 3 ch1 and turn (doesn't count as first st), 1dc into backloop only of each dc st, ss into next 2 sts from round 1. (4dc + 2ss)
Repeat rows 2–3 until all sts from round 1 have been worked into.
Fasten off and sew the ends of the ribbing together.

See page 38 for examples of ribbing. Repeat on the second arm hole.

Neck

Join yarn into sp where 2 triangles meet, shown with *on diagram.

Round 1 1dc into each st around the neck (2dc into the side of each tr st), until you are back where you started, ss into beg dc to join.

TIP
- The raw edge of the triangle has 16 sts.

Ribbing
Follow the same instructions as the arm hole ribbing.

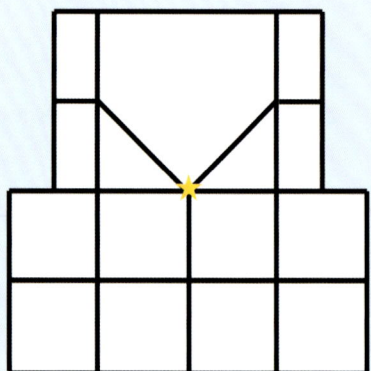

Hem

Join yarn into any st along the bottom hem.

Round 1 1dc into each st along the bottom hem, ss into beg dc to join.

TIP

- Each granny square has 17 sts.

Ribbing

The ribbing is worked in rows off round 1.

Row 1 ch7, 1dc into 2nd ch from hook, 1dc into each ch, ss into next 2 sts from round 1. (6dc + 2ss)

Row 2 Turn your work, then skip 2 ss, 1dc into backloop only of each dc st. (6dc)

Row 3 ch1 and turn (doesn't count as first st), 1dc into backloop only of each dc st, ss into next 2 sts from round 1. (6dc + 2ss)
Repeat rows 2–3 until all sts from round 1 have been worked into.

Fasten off and sew the ends of the ribbing together.

Sew in your ends and you are all done!

SKILL LEVEL

Love heart scrunchie

This scrunchie is for those days you just want to pull your hair back, but still feel great!

You will need:
- 5mm hook (or corresponding hook to reach gauge)
- A hair bobble or piece of elastic
- Aran yarn - approx 20g

Recommended yarn
Drops Air, wool mix
Yarn A   Inner colour 5g
Yarn B   Outer colour 15g

(Yarn quantities are based on average requirements for the yarn suggested and are therefore approximate measurements.)

Tension/gauge
Tension is not critical for this project, but it may affect the yarn quantities required. This design can be adapted to the size of the bobble/elastic uses. Any yarn weight will work for this design. I would recommend using a hook size suggested by the yarn. Change the number of stitches at the start to create the desired effect.

THIS PATTERN IS WRITTEN WITH U.K. TERMS
(Key: U.K. terms)

Ch = chain
Sp = space
St = stitch
Ss = slip stitch
Dc = double crochet
Tr = treble crochet
... = repeat instructions
Beg = beginning

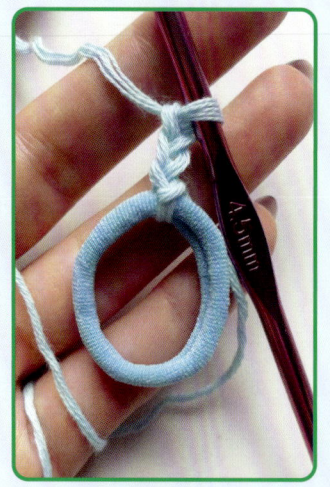

Round 1

Round 2

Round 3

Attach yarn A to bobble/elastic with a ss.

Round 1 ch3 (counts as first tr), working over the bobble/elastic, (2tr, ch1), then (3tr, ch1) working over the bobble/ elastic until the bobble is tightly filled with sts, ss into beg ch3 to join. (For me this is 75tr+ 25ch), **fasten off**.

Round 2 Join yarn B into any ch1 sp, ch3, (2tr, ch1, 3tr) into same ch1 sp, (ch1, 3tr, ch1, 3tr) into each ch1 sp, ch1 then ss into beg ch3 to join.

Round 3 ch1, skip st at base of ch1, *5tr into next st, skip next st, ss into ch1 sp, skip next st, 5tr into next st, skip next st, ss into ch1 sp, skip next st; repeat from * until end, **fasten off**.

Sew in the ends and you are done!

SKILL LEVEL

Retro flower bag

Whether you're popping out to the shops or taking your laptop to work, this bag will fit everything you need.

You will need:
- 10mm hook (or corresponding hook to reach gauge)
- Super chunky Yarn – approx 395g

Recommended yarn
Paintbox yarns, wool blend super chunky

Yarn A Navy Blue 5g
Yarn B Periwinkle 70g
Yarn C Emerald Green 320g

(Yarn quantities are based on average requirements for the yarn suggested and are therefore approximate measurements.)

Tension/gauge
Rounds 1-2 measure 10cm in diameter.

Finished measurements
Bag = 40cm X 40cm
Strap = 15cm X 50cm

THIS PATTERN IS WRITTEN WITH U.K. TERMS
(Key: U.K. terms)

Ch = chain
Sp = space
St = stitch
Ss = slip stitch
Dc = double crochet
Tr = treble crochet
... = repeat instructions
Beg = beginning

Changing yarn

You have to change the yarn colour frequently in this pattern. Please see page 82 for a detailed explanation of how to do this.

Front

Using Yarn A, make a magic ring

Round 1 ch3 (counts as first tr throughout), 11tr into ring, ss into top of beg ch3 to join, **fasten off**. (12tr)

Round 2 Using yarn B, join yarn into any st, ch3, 1tr into st at base of ch3, 1tr into next st, change to yarn C, 1tr into same st, change to yarn B, *2tr into next st, 1tr into next st, change to yarn C, 1tr into same st, change to yarn B; repeat from *around until end, ss in top beg ch3 to join. (24tr)

Round 3 ch3, 2tr into next st, 1tr into next st, change to yarn C, 2tr into next st, change to yarn B, *1tr into next st, 2tr into next st, 1tr into the next st, change to yarn C, 2tr into next st, change to yarn B; repeat from * around until end, ss into top of beg ch3 to join.(36tr)

Round 4 ch3, 1tr into next st, 2tr into next st, 1tr into next st, change to yarn C, 1tr into next st, 2tr into next st, change to yarn B, *1tr into next 2 sts, 2tr into next st, 1tr into next st, change to yarn C, 1tr into next st, 2tr into next st, change to yarn B; repeat from *around until end, ss into top of beg ch3 to join. (48tr)

Round 1

Round 2

Round 3

Round 5 ch3, 1tr into next 2 sts, 2tr into next st, 1tr into next st, change to yarn C, 1tr into the next 2 sts, 2tr into next st, change to yarn B, *1tr into the next 3 sts, 2tr into next st, 1tr into next st, change to yarn C, 1tr into the next 2 sts, 2tr into next st, change to yarn B; repeat from * around until end, ss into top of beg ch3 to join. (60tr)

Round 5

Round 6 ch1 (doesn't count as first st), 1dc into st at base of ch1, skip 2 sts, 7tr in between the sts, skip 2 sts, 1dc into the next st, change to yarn C, 1tr into the next 3 sts, 2tr into next st, *change to yarn B, 1dc into the next st, skip 2 sts, 7tr in between the sts, skip 2 sts, 1dc into the next st, change to yarn C, 1tr into the next 3 sts, 2tr into next st; repeat from * until end, ss into beg dc to join. **Fasten off yarn B**, continue with yarn C. (84sts)

Round 6

Round 7 ch3, 1tr into each st around until end, ss into top of beg ch3 to join. (84tr)

Round 8 ch3, 1tr into st at base of ch3, ch2, 2tr into next st, *1tr into next 19 sts, 2tr into next st, ch2, 2tr into next st; repeat from * 2 more times then 1tr into next 19 sts, ss into top of beg ch3 to join, **fasten off**. (92tr, 4 ch2 sps)

Round 8 (front complete)

OUT AND ABOUT IN THE CITY

Back

Using yarn C, make a magic ring.

Round 1 ch3 (counts as first tr throughout), 11tr into ring, ss into top of beg ch3 to join. (12tr)

Round 2 ch3, 1tr into st at base of ch3, 2tr into each st around, ss into top of beg ch3 to join. (24tr)

Round 3 ch3, 2tr into next st, *1tr into next st, 2tr into next st; repeat from * around until end, ss into top of beg ch3 to join. (36tr)

Round 4 ch3, 1tr into next st, 2tr into the next st, *1tr into next 2 sts, 2tr into next st; repeat from * around until end, ss into top of beg ch3 to join. (48tr)

Round 5 ch3, 1tr into next 2 sts, 2tr into next st, *1tr into next 3 sts, 2tr into next st; repeat from * around until end, ss into top of beg ch3 to join. (60 tr)

Round 6 ch3, 1tr into next 3 sts, 2tr into next st, *1tr into next 4 sts, 2tr into next st; repeat from * around ss into top of beg ch3 to join. (72 tr)

Round 7 ch3, 1tr into next 4 sts, 2tr into the next st, *1tr into next 5 sts, 2tr into the next st; repeat from * around, ss into top of beg ch3 to join. (84 tr)

Round 8 ch3, 1tr into the st at base of ch3, ch2, 2tr into next st, *1tr into the next 19 sts, 2tr into next st, ch2, 2tr into next st; repeat from * 2 more times, then 1tr into next 19 sts, ss into top of beg ch3 to join, **fasten off**. (92tr, 4 ch2 sps)

Side/ Strap

Using yarn C, ch110, ss into beg ch to join and make a loop.

Round 1 ch3 (counts as first tr), 1tr into each ch around until end, ss into beg ch3 to join, **fasten off**. (110tr)

Round 8 (back complete)

Attaching the pieces

Join yarn A into the top left ch2 corner sp of your front square.

TIP
- *Make sure the flower is facing the way you want it to.*

Round 1 ch1 (doesn't count as first st), with your front piece and side/strap wrong sides together, going through all loops, dc the pieces together along 3 sides (1dc into ch2 sp, 1dc into next 23 sts, 2dc into ch2 sp, 1dc into next 23 sts, 2dc into ch2 sp, 1dc into next 23 sts, 1dc into ch2 sp), now 1dc into each st along the top edge of the bag, (1dc into ch2 sp, 1dc into next 23 sts, 1dc into ch2 sp), ss into beg dc, then turn and 1dc into each st around the strap, ss into first dc along the top edge of the bag to join, **fasten off**.
Repeat the same thing for the back piece. When doing this make sure to match the stitches.

Sew in your ends and you are all done!

Crochet is essential when you go on holiday! Lounge in the sun with the cutest hat and protect your sunglasses with a crocheted case. Use your 'Hold my Ruffle bag' for exploring in the day and the 'Daisy Chain bag' for the evening.

All out summer holiday

SKILL BUILDER

Changing yarn colour

Changing your yarn colour during a project is a great way to make patterns. Once you have mastered this skill, you will be able to make lots of retro flower patterns!

1. You have to change the yarn colour frequently in this pattern and here is how to do so.
2. Work the last stitch using the old yarn up to the stage where the next 'step' is to complete the stitch, this will be when you wrap the yarn around the hook and draw through all the loops on the hook. The stopping point in this pattern will be when there are only 2 loops on the hook.
3. Let the old colour of yarn drop to the wrong side of the work and pick up the new colour yarn, leaving the end of the new yarn on the wrong side of the work.
4. Wrap the new colour of yarn around the hook and complete the stitch using the new yarn.
5. Now work the next stitches using the new yarn, working over the tail of the old yarn so you can pick it back up later in the pattern.

SKILL LEVEL

Sunglasses case

Protect your sunglasses with a crocheted case. A great pattern for beginners, as you just need to know how to make a granny square!

You will need:
- 4mm hook (or corresponding hook to reach gauge)
- DK yarn – approx 30g'

Recommended yarn
Paintbox Yarns Cotton Mix DK
Yarn A Candy Pink 20g
Yarn B Love 10g

Tension/gauge
Each granny square after round 3 should measure approx 7cm X 7cm

Finished measurements
16cm X 8cm

THIS PATTERN IS WRITTEN WITH U.K. TERMS
(Key: U.K. terms)

Ch = chain
Sp = space
St = stitch
Ss = slip stitch
Dc = double crochet
Tr = treble crochet
... = repeat instructions
Beg = beginning

Granny square

Make a magic ring.

Round 1 ch4 (counts as first tr + ch1), * 1tr into ring, ch1; repeat from * 6 more times, ss into the 3rd ch of beg ch4 to join. **Fasten off**. (8tr + 8ch)

Round 2 Join new colour into any ch1 sp, ch3 (counts as first tr throughout), 2tr into same ch1 sp, ch1, (3tr, ch1) into each ch1 sp around, ss into top of beg ch3 to join. **Fasten off**. (24tr + 8ch)

Square 1 up to round 3. Join as you go with your next squares to create two 1 X 2 rectangles.

Round 3 (Join as you go) Join new colour into any ch1 sp, ch3, (2tr, ch2, 3tr) into same sp, ch1, *3tr into next ch1 sp, ch1, (3tr, ch2, 3tr) into next ch1 sp, ch1; repeat from * 2 times, 3tr into next ch1 sp, ch1, ss into top of beg ch3 to join. **Fasten off**.

Join 2 squares together (joining as you go) to create a rectangle. Make 2 of these.

Join as you go

1   Crochet first square to end of round 3 (square 1).
2   Crochet your next square to end of round 2 square 2).
3   round 3, start your square as normal-(ch3, 2tr).
4   ch1, ss into the adjoining corner of square 1, to join the two squares. Finish corner as usual with 3tr.
5   ss into next ch1 space of square 1. *3tr as usual into square 2, ss into next ch1 sp of square 1.
6   3tr as usual into square 1, ss into ch2 sp of square 2 (ch1, 3tr into same sp as previous 3tr of square 1), complete the square as you usually would.

1 x 2 rectangle

Joining the squares

Place the 2 rectangles wrong sides together, join yarn into ch2 corner sp and dc along 3 sides, leaving one short side open. Match the stitches, going through all loops.

Continue with the same yarn, ss into ch2 space of the of the front top square.

Rounds 1-2 ch3, 1tr into each stitch along the top of the case, ss into beg ch3 to join. Repeat once more, then **fasten off**. (26tr)

Cord

Pull out a length of yarn approx 80cm. Leave this long tail and attach the yarn to your hook with a slip knot. Wind off a smaller ball of the last colour used and work cord using two strands of the same colour held together as one. Make a ch50. **Fasten off**.

Alternatively, you can ch however many stitches you want your cord to be and work a dc st into each ch.

Once you have created your cord weave this in and out of the top row of tr sts.

Sew in the ends and you are done!

SKILL LEVEL

Summer flower top hat

Get ready to have the cutest hat around the pool! This pattern has 2 options, you can use hat wire to add structure to the brim or leave it out for a more relaxed look.

You will need:
- 4mm hook (or corresponding hook to reach gauge)
- Aran cotton yarn - approx 90g
- Approx 90cm of hat wire (optional)

Recommended yarn
Yarns & Colors, Epic, cotton Yarn
Yarn A (flower centre) - Mustard 5g
Yarn B (petals) - Cream 20g
Yarn C (main hat colour) - Cotton Candy 70g

(Yarn quantities are based on average requirements for the yarn suggested and are therefore approximate measurements.)

Tension/gauge
After round 4 = 10cm X 10cm

Finished measurements
50cm around, 23cm length

THIS PATTERN IS WRITTEN WITH U.K. TERMS
(Key: U.K. terms)
Ch = chain
Sp = space
St = stitch
Ss = slip stitch
Dc = double crochet
Tr = treble crochet
... = repeat instructions
Beg = beginning

Changing yarn

You have to change the yarn colour frequently in this pattern. Please see page 82 for a detailed explanation of how to do this.

Round 6

Round 7

Round 15

Hat

This hat is worked from the top down.

Using yarn A, make a magic ring.

Round 1 ch3 (counts as first tr throughout), 11tr into ring, ss into top of beg ch3 to join, **fasten off**. (12tr)

Round 2 Using yarn B, join yarn into any st, ch3, 1tr into st at base of ch3, 1tr into next st, change to yarn C, 1tr into the same st, *change to yarn B, 2tr into next st, 1tr into next st, change to yarn C, 1tr into the same st, repeat from * 4 more times, change to yarn B, ss in top beg ch3 to join. (24tr)

Round 3 ch3, 2tr into next st, 1tr into next st, change to yarn C, 2tr into next st, *change to yarn B, 1tr into the next st, 2tr into next st, 1tr into the next st, change to yarn C, 2tr into next st; repeat from * around until end, change to yarn B, ss into top of beg ch3 to join. (36tr)

Round 4 ch3, 1tr into next st, 2tr into next st, 1tr into next st, change to yarn C, 1tr into next st, 2tr into next st, *change to yarn B, 1tr into next 2 sts, 2tr into next st, 1tr into next st, change to yarn C, 1tr into the next st, 2tr into next st; repeat from * around until end, change to yarn B, ss into top of beg ch3 to join. (48tr)

Round 5 ch3, 1tr into next 2 sts, 2tr into next st, 1tr into next st, change to yarn C, 1tr into next 2 sts, 2tr into next st, change to yarn B, *1tr into the next 3 sts, 2tr into the next st, 1tr into next st, change to yarn C, 1tr into next 2 sts, 2tr into next st, change to yarn B; repeat from * around until end, ss into top of beg ch3 to join. (60tr)

Round 6 ch3, 1tr into next 3 sts, 2tr into next st, 1tr into next st, change to yarn C, 1tr into next 3 sts, 2tr into next st, change to yarn B, *1tr into next 4 sts, 2tr into next st, 1tr into next st, change to yarn C, 1tr into next 3 sts, 2tr into next st, change to yarn B; repeat from * around until end, ss into top of beg ch3 to join. (72tr)

Round 7 ch1 (doesn't count as first dc st), 1dc into st at base of ch1, skip 2 sts, 7tr into next st, skip 2 sts, 1dc into next st, change to yarn C, 1tr into next 5 sts, *change to yarn B, 1dc into next st, skip 2 sts, 7tr into next st, skip 2 sts, 1dc into the next st, change to yarn C, 1tr into next 5 sts; repeat from *until end, ss into top of beg dc to join. **Fasten off yarn B**, continue with yarn C. (84sts)

Rounds 8-15 ch3, 1tr into each st until end, ss into top of ch3 to join. (84tr)

TIP
- *You may find you need more/less rows, depending on your tension/head size. Try your hat on and adjust the rows accordingly.*

Round 20

Round 16 ch2 (counts as first htr st), working into the front loops only 1htr into the next 5 sts, then *2htr into next st, 1htr into next 6 sts; repeat from * until end, ss into top of beg ch2 to join. (96htr)

Round 17 ch2, 1htr into next 6 sts, then *2htr into next st, 1htr into next 7 sts; repeat from * until end, ss into top of beg ch2 to join. (108htr)

Round 18 ch2, 1htr into next 7 sts, then *2htr into next st, 1htr into next 8 sts; repeat from * until end, ss into top of beg ch2 to join. (120htr)

Round 19 ch2, 1htr into next 8 sts, then *2htr into next st, 1htr into next 9 sts; repeat from * until end, ss into top of beg ch2 to join. (132htr)

Round 20 ch2, 1htr into next 9 sts, then *2htr into the next st, 1htr into next 10 sts; repeat from * until end, ss into top of beg ch2 to join. **Fasten off here if you don't want to add wire.** (144htr)

Adding wire to the brim (optional)

Place the brim of the hat onto a flat surface and measure how long you need your wire. It should be very slightly bigger than the brim. (Mine was 90cm of wire).

Round 21 ch1, crocheting over the wire, *1dc into next st, 2dc into next st; repeat from * around to end, ss to beg dc to join.
Fasten off. (216dc)

Sew in the end and you are all done!

Work over the wire to attach it to your hat.

Hold my ruffle bag

SKILL LEVEL

The ideal bag for exploring on holiday. Wear with your favourite shorts, a cute top and some sandals.

You will need:
- 5mm hook
- Aran, cotton yarn - approx 250g

Recommended yarn
Yarn and colors Epic, Cotton, Aran
Yarn A 160g
Yarn B 30g
Yarn C 60g

(Quantities are based on average requirements and are therefore approximate measurements.)

THIS PATTERN IS WRITTEN WITH U.K. TERMS
(Key: U.K. terms)

Ch = chain
Sp = space
St = stitch
Ss = slip stitch
Dc = Double crochet
Tr = Treble crochet
Tr2tog = Treble crochet 2 stitches together (decrease)
... = repeat instructions
Beg = beginning

YARN A - ORCHID
YARN B - CARDINAL
YARN C - LIME

YARN A - PEONY LEAF
YARN B - VIOLET
YARN C - OPALINE GLASS

Tension/Gauge
10cm X 10cm = 14 sts X 9 rows
(of 1 row dc, 3 rows tr repeated)

Finished measurements
42cm X 40cm

TIPS
- *For this design it doesn't matter too much if your tension isn't the same but keep in mind, if your gauge is coming out smaller than suggested your finished bag will be smaller. If your gauge is coming out bigger, your finished bag will be bigger.*
- *Keep in mind that if your gauge swatch is smaller the bag strap may not be long enough to wear over the shoulder.*

Gauge swatch

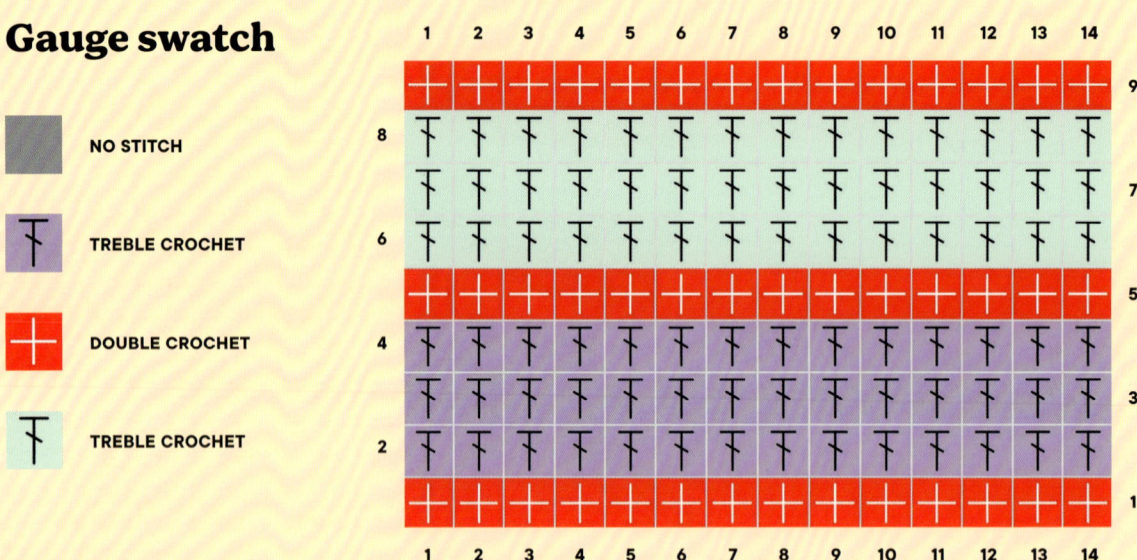

Strap
The bag is worked by first creating 2 straps and then working the bag continuously onto the straps.

TIPS
- *I recommend you starting chain measures around 50cm (before joining to make a loop). If your starting ch is too small add a few more chains. Do less chains if it is too big.*
- *Work over the chain not into the stitches, like you do when starting a granny square.*
- *Push up the stitches so you can fit them in and try to make them as evenly spaced as you can.*

Using yarn A ch60, ss into beg ch to join and make a loop.

Round 1 ch1, working OVER the ch (not into the sts), 160dc, make sure your sts are not twisted, ss into beg dc to join. (160dc)

Round 2 ch5 (counts as 1tr + ch2), 1tr into next 100 sts, ch2, 1tr into next 59 sts, ss into 3rd ch of beg ch5 to join. (160tr + 4ch)

Round 3 ss into ch2 sp, ch5 (counts as 1tr + ch2), 2tr into ch2 sp, 1tr into next 100 sts, (2tr, ch2, 2tr) into ch2 sp, 1tr into next 60 sts, 1tr into ch2 sp, ss into 3rd ch of beg ch5 to join. (168tr + 4ch)

Round 4 ss into ch2 sp, ch5 (counts as 1tr + ch2), 2tr into ch2 sp, 1tr into next 104 sts, (2tr, ch2, 2tr) into ch2 sp, 1tr into next 64 sts, 1tr into ch2 sp, ss into 3rd ch of beg ch5 to join, **fasten off**. (176tr + 4ch)

Make 2 of these straps.

Strap 1
Join yarn B into right ch2 sp.

Round 5 ch1, 1dc into ch2 sp, 1dc into next 108 sts, (1dc, ch2, 1dc) into ch2 sp (add a stitch maker into ch2 sp), 1dc into next 68 sts, (1dc, ch2) into ch2 sp, ss into beg dc to join (add a stitch maker into ch2 sp), **fasten off**. (180dc + 4ch)

Strap 2
Join yarn B into right ch2 sp.

Round 5 ch1, 1dc into ch2 sp, 1dc into next 108 sts, (1dc, ch1) into ch2 sp, ss into bottom right ch2 sp of strap 1, ch1, working into strap 2, 1dc into ch2 sp, 1dc into next 68 sts, (1dc, ch1) into ch2 sp, (make sure the 2 straps are not twisted), ss into left ch2 corner sp of strap 1, ch1, ss into beg dc to join, **fasten off**. (180dc + 4ch)

You will make 2 straps like this, then with round 5 of strap 2, you will join the 2 strap together.

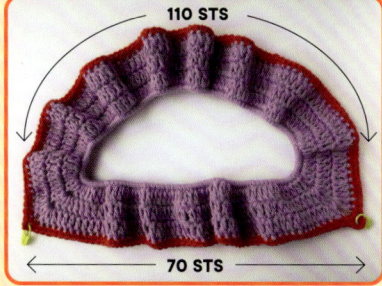

Top from corner to corner 110 sts Bottom from corners 70 sts

Body of the bag

Join yarn C into the bottom left ch2 corner sp of one of the straps, (working along the short side of the straps with 70 sts from corner to corner).

Round 1 ch3 (counts as first tr st throughout), 1tr into next 70 sts, 1tr into ch2 sp, now working into the 2nd strap, 1tr into ch2 sp, 1tr into next 70 sts, 1tr into into ch2 sp, ss into beg ch-3 to join. (144tr)

Round 2 ch3 and turn, 1tr into next 3 sts, tr2tog, *1tr into next 4 sts, tr2tog; repeat from * around, ss into beg ch3 to join. (120tr)

Round 3 ch3 and turn, 1tr into each st around, ss into beg ch3 to join, **fasten off**. (120tr)

Round 4 Join yarn B into any st (I suggest always joining into the side to keep it neat), 1dc into each st around, ss into beg dc to join, **fasten off**. (120dc)

Round 5 Join yarn A into any st (I suggest always joining into the side to keep it neat), ch3, 1tr into each st around, ss into beg ch3 to join. (120tr)

Rounds 6-7 ch3 and turn, 1tr into each st around, ss into beg ch3 to join, **fasten off after round 7**. (120tr)

Round 8 Join yarn B into any st, 1dc into each st around, ss into beg dc to join, **fasten off**. (120dc)

Round 9 Join yarn C into any st, ch3, 1tr into each st around, ss into beg ch3 to join. (120tr)

Rounds 10-11 ch3 and turn, 1tr into each st around, ss into beg ch3 to join, **fasten off after round 11**. (120tr)

Round 12 Join yarn B into any st, 1dc into each st around, ss into beg dc to join, **fasten off**. (120dc)

Round 13 Join yarn A into any st, ch3, 1tr into each st around, ss into beg ch3 to join. (120dc)

Rounds 14-15 ch3 and turn, 1tr into each st around, ss into beg ch3 to join, **fasten off after round 15**. (120tr)

Round 16 Join yarn B into any st, 1dc into each st around, ss into beg dc to join, **fasten off**. (120dc)

Sewing up the bottom

Lay the bag out flat and use stitch markers to mark out which stitches to match up when sewing up the bottom. Because of the way crochet can twist when working up it might not be that where you fastened off is the best place to start.

Using a mattress stitch sew up the bottom of the bag matching the stitches. You should have 60 sts on each side.

Sewing up the side

To add a little more structure to the bag, sew together the 2 straps at the top of the bag. Sew up 8 sts with a mattress st.

Sew in your ends and you are all done!

Daisy chain bag

SKILL LEVEL

Inspired by daisy chains you used to make when you were little, individual flowers crocheted together to make the prettiest bag.

You will need:
- 5mm hook (or corresponding hook to reach gauge)
- Cotton aran yarn - approx 100g
- Approx ½ metre of fabric for lining (You will see this through the crocheted bag, keep this in mind when choosing your fabric)

Recommended yarn
Yarn and Colors Epic, Cotton, Aran
Yarn A   Mustard - a small amount
Yarn B   Cream - 100g

Any aran yarn will work for this pattern making it a perfect project for using up your stash! Lighter weight and chunkier yarn will work too but it may affect the size/look of the bag.

Tension/gauge
Each flower = 8cm

Create one flower and measure across the centre from the tip of the flower petal to the tip of the opposite flower petal.

TIP
- *Tension is not critical for this project, but keep in mind, if your flowers are smaller your bag will be smaller and vice versa.*

Finished measurements
Bag = 21cm X 18cm   Strap = 40cm

THIS PATTERN IS WRITTEN WITH U.K. TERMS
(Key: U.K. terms)

Ch = chain
Sp = space
St = stitch
Ss = slip stitch
Dc = double crochet
Dtr = double treble crochet
... = repeat instructions
Beg = beginning

Construction

You will be attaching your flowers as you go. Most of the bag uses the '6 petal flower' (use this flower to check gauge) but you will need X 2 '5 petal flowers' to start/end the strap.

Round 1

I highly recommend reading through the whole pattern before starting. The bag is worked from the top down and then you will add the strap.

Create your first '6 petal flower'.

6 petal flower

This flower motif is used for most of the bag. This is how to make the flowers and you will be attaching them as you go. Create 1 flower first, from then on you will be attaching them as you go.

If you would like your flower centre to be different than your petals, use yarn A for round 1 and yarn B for round 2.

ch4, ss into beg ch1 to join and make a ring.

Round 1 ch1 (doesn't count as 1st st), 12dc into ring, ss into first dc to join. (12dc)

Round 2 *ch3, 3dtr into next st, ch3, ss into next st; repeat from *5 more times, working your last ss into the same st you started, **fasten off.**

Now, joining as you go, create 4 more flowers attaching them to create a chain of 5 flowers.

First 6 petal flowers

Join as you go to create a 5 flower chain

Joining the flowers

TIPS
- *When attaching the flowers make sure they are always front-facing.*
- *I recommend crocheting as many petals as you can before joining (for example, if you need to attach 3 petals, crochet 3 petals before joining).*
- *When referring to orange and purple flowers, I am referring to the images to the right.*

Complete one flower (orange). Then crochet a second flower (purple) up to the petal you would like to join to the completed (orange) flower.

ch3, dtr into next st, take your hook out of the (purple) flower. Insert your hook into the middle dtr st of the petal of the (orange) flower you are joining to. Reinsert your hook into the loop of the working (purple) flower and pull through the loop.

2dtr into same st as first dtr of the (purple) flower, like you normally would. Complete the flower like you normally would.

To attach the flowers to more than one flower follow the same steps, stacking the flowers like bricks.

Insert your hook into the flower you are joining to.

Reinsert your hook into the loop of the working flower.

Pull through the loop.

Complete the petal as normal.

Finish your flower like normal and now your 2 flowers are attached.

With your 6th flower; crochet 2 petals, with your 3rd petal attach to the chain of flowers like before, crochet 2 more petals, then with your 6th petal, join to the first flower (into the petal opposite the petal you first attached to) to connect the chain.

Round 2

You will be stacking your flowers like bricks for round 2.

Flower 1 With your first flower join to 2 petals, 1 into each of the 2 flowers above.

Flowers 2-5 You will be attaching these flowers with 3 petals. 1 into each of the 2 flowers above. 1 into the flower to the side.

Flower 6 You will be attaching this flower with 4 petals. 1 into the first flower of round 2. 1 into each of the 2 flowers above. 1 into the flower to the side.

TIPS

- Simply; for rounds 1 and 2, attach your flowers so you have a 6 X 2 flower tube.
- Round 2 will have folded flowers at either side. Rounds 1 and 3 you will see 3 complete flowers when laid out flat. This is important for when you join the bottom of the bag.

Round 2
- flower 1

Round 2
- flowers 2–5

Round 2
- complete

Round 3

You will continue to stack your flowers like bricks for round 3. Attach the first 3 flowers like you have done previously. With the next 3 flowers (flowers 4-6), you will also be attaching the flowers with the bottom 2 petals, to the first 3 flowers bottom 2 petals, the flowers will sit directly on top of one another. This seals the bottom of the bag.

Flowers 1-3 Attach 3 flowers in the same way as round 2.

You will now be attaching the flowers like before but also attaching at the bottom. This can be a little fiddly, you may want to use some stitch markers to mark which petals you will be working into.

Flowers 4-5 You will be attaching these flowers with 5 petals. 1 into each of the 2 flowers above. 3 into the flower to the side (1 into the side like usual, then attach the 2 bottom petals to the 2 bottom petals).

Flower 6 You will be attaching this flower with 6 petals. 1 into each of the 2 flowers above. 4 into the flower to the side (1 into the side like usual, then attach the 2 bottom petals to the 2 bottom petals, then 1 into the other side petal).

End of round 3

The position of the flowers should look the same on both sides. The lines show which petals are attached to one another. The flowers should sit directly on top of one another. The red lines show where they will be attached to the same petal of the flower on the other side.

ALL OUT SUMMER HOLIDAY 105

Strap

To create the strap you need 2 X '5 petal flowers' one to start and one to end the strap. You will be 'joining as you go' like before.

Join the 5 petal flower at the top on the side of the bag into 2 petals, 1 into the flower at the front and 1 into the flower at the back.

5 petal flower

ch4, ss into beg ch1 to join and make a ring.

Round 1 ch1 (doesn't count as 1st st), 10dc into ring, ss into first dc to join. (10dc)

Round 2 *ch3, 1dtr into next st, join into petal at top corner of bag, 2dtr in same st, ch3, ss in next st; repeat from * once more to join the next petal to the other flower at the top corner, (ch3, 3dtr in next st, ch3, ss in next st) 3 times. **Fasten off**.

Repeat on the other side of the bag.

Now go back to using a '6 petal flower'. Join as many flowers as you wish, to create the strap length you want. I suggest a total of 5 flowers for a short strap. With your last flower, attach on 2 opposite sides to join the strap together.

Sew in your ends before adding the lining

Lining the bag

Measure the size of your bag; lay the bag out flat and measure from the 'top to bottom' and from 'side to side'. Cut out 4 rectangles of lining fabric to these measurements with a 1cm seam allowance. (I like to use a heavy weight fabric to give the bag more structure).

Place 2 rectangles together, right sides together and sew along 3 sides leaving the top edge open.

Repeat this with your other 2 rectangles.

Press/iron the 1cm seam allowance edge on both pieces.

Turn one of your lining pieces right side out and with the second lining wrong side out, place that lining into the first. Pin the 2 pieces together along the top edge.

As you have pressed your hem along the top, you should now have a neat edge. 'Top stitch' along the edge, to attach the 2 lining pieces together.

Insert the pouch into the bag and tack the bag to the lining with a few stitches.

You are going to need these crocheted pieces when it gets colder outside. A crocheted jumper to keep you warm, as well as a hat, scarf and mittens. Make these in the same yarn, and you will have a cute matching set.

Cosy winter vibes

SKILL BUILDER

Finishing your pieces

Once the crochet is done, there are a few things to do to finish off your piece. These tips will help to make your pieces look, fit and feel the best they can!

Blocking

Blocking is used to relax the fibres and make the piece sit in the position you want it to. There are a few ways to block your pieces. Some patterns may require you to block individual parts/squares before assembling and others may suggest blocking the piece once it is finished.

Wet blocking is done by using some gentle degertent and soaking the piece in warm water for 30 mins. Rinse and drain the water, squeeze out as much water as you can but do not ring out the piece. Place the piece on a dry towel and roll up the towel with the piece inside. Squeeze it to get as much water out as possible. Place the piece onto blocking matts (or you can use a towel) and pin (using rust free pins) into place, following the measurements provided. Leave to air dry completely before unpinning.

For synthetic fibres like acrylic, steaming will work better. Pin the piece out into the measurements required and use a steamer to lightly run over the piece. Leave to air dry completely before unpinning.

To block granny squares, pin the squares into the measurements required or you can use a wooden blocking board. Spray the squares with water and leave to air dry completely before unpinning.

Sewing in your ends

I recommend leaving quite a big tail when fastening off your work. This allows you to easily sew in your ends so nothing comes undone. Using a sewing needle with a large eye, thread your end. Use the rule of 3 to pass the yarn back and forth 3 times into the back of your work.

I recommend sewing in your ends as you go to make it more enjoyable. Having lots of ends to sew in once the project is finished can be boring. However, make sure what you have done is correct before sewing in an end; it will be much harder to frog a piece if you have already sewn the end in.

Retro flower scarf

SKILL LEVEL

Wrap up in this cosy scarf. Make it in one solid colour or go for stripes to make it even more fun.

You will need:
- 5mm hook (or corresponding hook to reach gauge)
- Aran yarn - approx 205g

Recommended yarn
Any aran yarn will work for this pattern *(Yarn quantities are based on average requirements for Yarn and Colors Epic yarn and are therefore approximate measurements, using different yarn may effect the amount needed.)*

Tension/gauge
Granny square (after round 6)= 15cm X 15cm
14 sts X 7 rows of tr st = 10cm X 10cm

Finished measurements
15cm X 165cm

OPTION 1 - SOLID COLOUR
STYLECRAFT SPECIAL, ACRYLIC
YARN A - GOLD 5G
YARN B - CREAM 20G
YARN C - PISTACHIO 180G

OPTION 2 – STRIPES
YARN & COLORS EPIC, COTTON
YARN A – LIME 80G
YARN B – BORDEAUX 40G
YARN C – THISTLE 85G

THIS PATTERN IS WRITTEN WITH U.K. TERMS
(Key: U.K. terms)

Ch = chain
Sp = space
St = stitch
Ss = slip stitch
Dc = double crochet
htr = half treble crochet
Tr = treble crochet
...= repeat instructions
Beg= beginning

Changing yarn

You have to change the yarn colour frequently in this pattern. Please see page 82 for a detailed explanation of how to do this.

Flower granny square

Using yarn A, make a magic ring

Round 1 ch3 (counts as first tr throughout), 11tr into ring, ss into top of beg ch3 to join, **fasten off**. (12tr)

Round 2 Using yarn B, join yarn into any st, ch3 (counts as first tr throughout), 1tr into st at base of ch3, 1tr into next st, change to yarn C, 1tr into the same st, change to yarn B, *2tr into next st, 1tr into next st, change to yarn C, 1tr into the same st, change to yarn B; repeat from * until end ss in top beg ch3 to join. (24tr)

Round 3 ch3, 2tr into next st, 1tr into next st, change to yarn C, 2tr into next st, change to yarn B, *1tr into next st, 2tr into next st, 1tr into next st, change to yarn C, 2tr into next st, change to yarn B; repeat from * around until end, ss into top of beg ch3 to join. (36 tr)

Round 4 ch1 (doesn't count as first dc), skip st at base of ch1 and skip next st, work 5tr in between sts, skip next st, 1dc into next st, change to yarn C, 1tr into next st, 2tr into next st, *change to yarn B, 1dc into next st, skip next st, then 5tr in between sts, skip next st, 1dc into the next st, change to yarn C, 1tr into the next st, 2tr into next st; repeat from * until end, ss into beg tr to join. **Fasten off yarn B, continue with yarn C.**

Round 5 ch3, 1tr into the stitch at base of ch3,

Side 1 - ch2, 2htr into next stitch, 1htr into next 11sts, 2htr into next st.

Side 2 - *ch2, 2tr into next st, skip dc st, 1tr into next 3 sts, skip dc st, 1htr into next st, 1dc into next 3 sts, 1htr into next st, skip dc st, 1tr into next 3 sts,* skip dc st, 2tr into next st.

Side 3 - Repeat 'side 1'.

Side 4 - Repeat from *-* of 'side 2', then ss into beg ch3 to join.

Round 6 ch3 (counts as first st), 1tr into next st, *(2tr, ch2, 2tr) into ch2 sp, 1tr into next 15 sts; repeat from *2 more times, then (2tr, ch2, 2tr) into ch2 sp, 1tr into next 13 sts, ss into top of beg ch3 to join, **fasten off**.

Make 2 flower squares

Side 1

Side 2

Round 5

Round 6

Join yarn into the ch2 corner of one of your squares (make sure the flower is facing the way you want it to).

Row 1 ch3 (counts as first tr throughout), 1tr into next 19 sts, 1tr into ch2 sp. (21tr)

Rows 2-78 ch3 and turn, 1tr into each st until end, **fasten off after row 78**. (21tr)

It is up to you when you change yarn colour, if you do at all.
Suggested colour changes (repeat until you have worked 78 rows):
1 Row   Yarn B
10 Rows   Yarn A
1 Row   Yarn B
10 Rows   Yarn C

Row 1

Sew the 2nd square to row 78.

TIPS
- *If you want your scarf to be longer, add more rows.*
- *Leave a long enough tail so that you can sew the other square to the end of this piece.*
- *If your edges aren't coming out straight when doing ch3, try ch2 at the start of each row instead.*

Using a mattress stitch, sew the second square to the other end of the scarf (make sure the flower is facing the same way as the first).

Sew in the ends and you are all done!

COSY WINTER VIBES 119

SKILL LEVEL

Retro flower jumper

This is my all-time favourite jumper! It is designed to be tight-fitting and cropped, but make it a few sizes bigger for an oversized fit.

You will need:
- 7mm hook (or corresponding hook to reach gauge)
- 5mm hook (or hook 2 sizes smaller than the hook used to reach gauge)
- Chunky yarn

Recommended yarn
Drops, Melody (main colour)
Yarn C Powder Pink

You only need a small amount for the flower so it is a great time to use up some of your scrap yarn. It doesn't have to be the same brand used for the body but it still needs to be a chunky weight.

Paintbox yarn simply chunky (flower)
Yarn A Mustard Yellow
Yarn B Rose Red

THIS PATTERN IS WRITTEN WITH U.K. TERMS
(Key: U.K. terms)

Ch = chain
Sp = space
St = stitch
Ss = slip stitch
Dc = double crochet
htr = half treble crochet
Tr = treble crochet
Fptr = front post treble crochet
Tr2tog = treble crochet 2 together
Dc2tog = double crochet 2 stitches together
... = repeat instructions
Beg = beginning
Yo = Yarn over hook

Tension/gauge

The body of the jumper is made with a 7mm hook or equivalent to get the right tension. The hem, cuff and neck are done with a 5mm hook (or approx 2 sizes small than the size used for the body/sleeves).

Square size after round 8 = 25cm X 25cm (once blocked)

10cm X 10cm = 6 rows X 11 sts, tr stitches (once blocked)

Sizing

This is a tight-fitting piece; keep this in mind when choosing which size to go for. If you want something more oversized go up a size or two.

To measure your bust/chest, measure around the fullest part of your bust.

	XS	S	M	L	XL	2XL	3XL	4XL	5XL
To fit chest/Bust (cm)	71-76	81-86	91.5-96.5	101.5-106.5	111.5-117	122-127	132-137	142-147	152-158
Finished circumference, after blocking (cm)	76	82	90	106	120	128	140	150	156
Finished length, after blocking (cm)	43	45	47	54	59	63	69	74	74
Sleeve length (plus cuff), after blocking (cm)	57	58	58	59	59	60	60	62	62

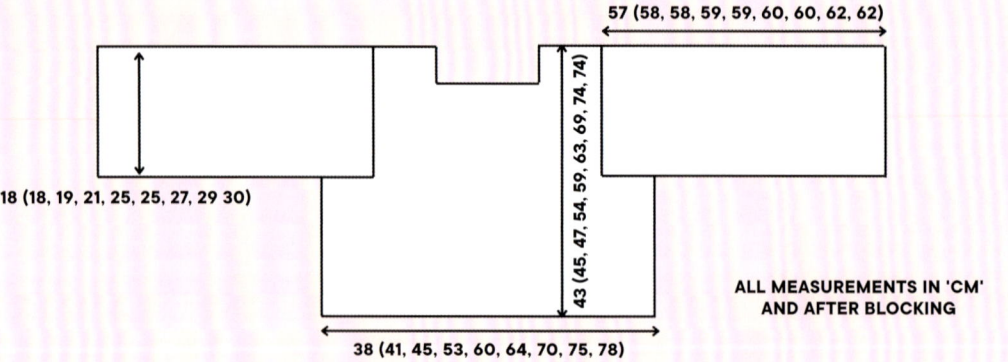

57 (58, 58, 59, 59, 60, 60, 62, 62)

43 (45, 47, 54, 59, 63, 69, 74, 74)

18 (18, 19, 21, 25, 25, 27, 29 30)

38 (41, 45, 53, 60, 64, 70, 75, 78)

ALL MEASUREMENTS IN 'CM' AND AFTER BLOCKING

Yarn quantities

Quantities for each size are shown in the table. They are based on average requirements, using the yarn suggested, and are therefore approximate measurements. Other yarns will work but it may affect the amount of yarn needed.

TIP
- The 'metres' used are a more accurate measurement when using different yarns than suggested.

	XS	S	M	L	XL	2XL	3XL	4XL	5XL
Yarn A (flower centre)	1g/2m	1g/2m	1g/2m	1g/2m	1g/2m	1g/2m	1g/2m	1g/2m	1g/2m
Yarn B (flower)	20g/28m	20g/28m	20g/28m	20g/28m	20g/28m	20g/28m	20g/28m	20g/28m	20g/28m
Yarn C (main colour)	235g/660m	240g/670m	250g/700m	325g/910m	400g/1115m	435g/1215m	480g/1340m	535g/1495m	580g/1630m

Jumper construction

The jumper is made by creating a square for the front and back. You will then add on the side tabs and top tabs. Once you have created the front and back pieces you will sew them together along the side tabs and the top tabs. Sizes XS, S, M & L, you will add extra rows to the length. The sleeves are then worked in the round onto the body.

Size XS, S, M, L

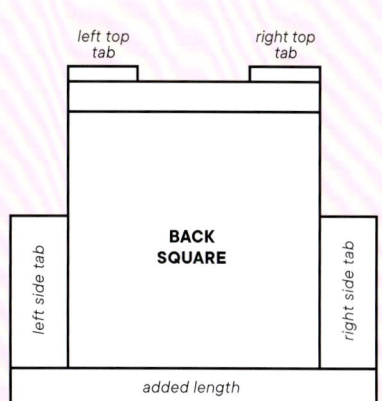

Size XL, 2XL

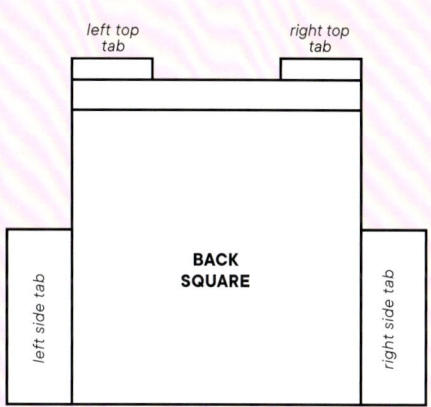

Size 3XL, 4XL, 5XL

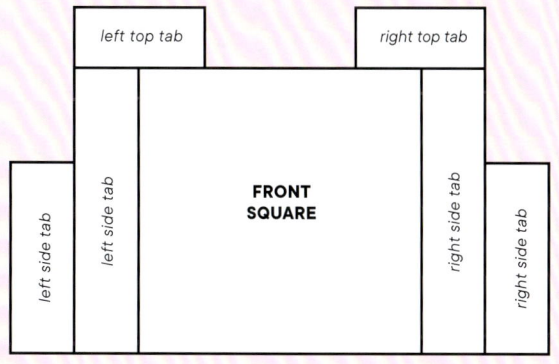
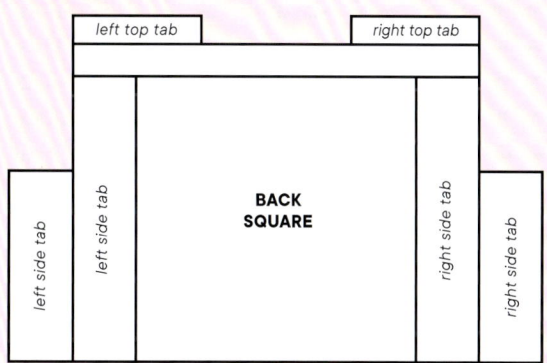

Changing yarn

You have to change the yarn colour frequently in this pattern. Please see page 82 for a detailed explanation of how to do this.

Front square

Using yarn A, make a magic ring. (Alternatively you can ch4 and ss into 1st ch to join and make a ring.)

Round 1 ch3 (counts as first tr throughout), 11tr into ring, ss into top of beg ch3 to join, **fasten off.** (12tr)

Round 2 Using yarn B, join yarn into any st, ch3, 1tr into st at base of ch3, 1tr into next st, change to yarn C, 1tr into the same st, *change to yarn B, 2tr into next st, 1tr into next st, change to yarn C, 1tr into the same st; repeat from * 4 more times, change to yarn B, ss into top of beg ch3 to join. (24tr)

Round 3 ch3, 2tr into next st, 1tr into next st, change to yarn C, 2tr into next st, *change to yarn B, 1tr into next st, 2tr into next st, 1tr into next st, change to yarn C, 2tr into next st; repeat from * 4 more times, change to yarn B, ss into beg ch3 to join. (36tr)

Round 4 ch3, 1tr into next st, 2tr into next st, 1tr into next st, change to yarn C, 1tr into next st, 2tr into next st, *change to yarn B, 1tr into next 2 sts, 2tr into next st, 1tr into next st, change to yarn C, 1tr into next st, 2tr into next st; repeat from * 4 more times, change to yarn B, ss into top of beg ch3 to join. (48tr)

Round 5 ch3, 1tr into next 2 sts, 2tr into next st, 1tr into next st, change to yarn C, 1tr into the next 2 sts, 2tr into next st, change to yarn B, *1tr into next 3 sts, 2tr into next st, 1tr into next st, change to yarn C, 1tr into next 2 sts, 2tr into next st, change to yarn B; repeat from * 4 more times, ss into top of beg ch3 to join. (60tr)

Round 6 Skip the st you have just ss into, then skip next 2 sts, 7tr in between sts, skip 2 sts, 1dc into next st, change to yarn C, 1tr into next 3 sts, 2tr into the next st, *change to yarn B, 1dc into next st, skip 2 sts, 7tr in between sts, skip 2 sts, 1dc into next st, change to yarn C, 1tr into next 3 sts, 2tr into next st; repeat from * 4 more times, ss into beg tr to join, **fasten off yarn B**, continue with yarn C. (83sts)

Round 7 ch3, 1tr into the stitch at base of ch3.

Side 1 - ch2, 2htr into the next stitch, 1htr into next 17 sts, 2htr into next st.

Side 2 - *ch2, 2tr into next st, skip dc st from previous round, 1tr into next 5 sts, skip dc st from previous round, 1tr into next st, 1htr into next st, 1dc into the next 3 sts, 1htr into next st, 1tr into next st, skip dc st from previous round, 1tr into next 5 sts,* skip dc st from previous round, 2tr into next st.

Side 3 - Repeat 'side 1'.

Side 4 - Repeat from *-* of 'side 2' then ss into top of beg ch3 to join (each side should have 21sts).

Round 8 ch3 and turn, 1tr into next 19 sts, *(2tr, ch2, 2tr) into ch2 sp, 1tr into next 21 sts; repeat from * 2 more times, then (2tr, ch2, 2tr) into ch2 sp, 1tr into next st, ss into top of beg ch3 to join. (100tr)

Round 9 ch3 and turn your work, *1tr into each st until ch2 sp, (2tr, ch2, 2tr) into ch2 sp; repeat from * 3 more times, then 1tr into each st until end, ss into top of beg ch3 to join. Repeat round 9 until 9 (10, 11, 13, 15, 16, 17, 18, 18) rounds have been worked, then **fasten off.**

Size of square after final round, once blocked (cm) 28 (31, 35, 43, 50, 54, 60, 65, 65)

Round 5

Round 6

Round 7 - side 1

Round 7 - side 2

Round 7

Front square (image shows a size M)

COSY WINTER VIBES 125

Back square

Using yarn C, make a magic ring.

Round 1 ch3 (counts as first tr throughout), 11tr into ring, ss into top of beg ch3 to join. (12tr)

Round 2 ch3, 1tr into st at base of ch3, 2tr into each st around, ss into top beg ch3 to join. (24tr)

Round 3 ch3 and turn, 2tr into next st, *1tr into next st, 2tr into next st; repeat from * around until end, ss into top of beg ch3 to join. (36tr)

Round 4 ch3 and turn, 1tr into next st, 2tr into next st, *1tr into next 2 sts, 2tr into next st; repeat from * around until end, ss into top of beg ch3 to join. (48tr)

Round 5 ch3 and turn, 1tr into next 2 sts, 2tr into next st, *1tr into next 3 sts, 2tr into next st; repeat from * around until end, ss into top of beg ch3 to join. (60tr)

Round 6 ch3 and turn, 1tr into next 3 sts, 2tr into next st, *1tr into next 4 sts, 2tr into next st; repeat from * around ss into top of beg ch3 to join. (72tr)

Round 7 ch3 and turn, 1tr into next 4 sts, 2tr into next st, *1tr into next 5 sts, 2tr into next st; repeat from * around, ss into top of beg ch3 to join. (84tr)

Round 8 ch3 and turn, *3tr into next st, ch2, 3tr into next st, 1tr into next 19 sts; repeat from * 2 more times, then 3tr into next st, ch2, 3tr into next st, 1tr into next 18 sts, ss into top of beg ch3 to join. (100tr)

Round 9 ch3 and turn, *1tr into each st until ch2 sp, (2tr, ch2, 2tr) into ch2 sp; repeat from * 3 more times, then 1tr into each st until end, ss into top of beg ch3 to join. Repeat round 9 until 9 (10, 11, 13, 15, 16, 17, 18, 18) have been worked, then **fasten off**

Size of square after final round, once blocked (cm) 28 (31, 35, 43, 50, 54, 60, 65, 65)

Back square (image shows a size M)

Adding width (SIZES 3XL, 4XL & 5XL ONLY)

Right side

SIZES 3XL, 4XL & 5XL ONLY
With your work facing the front, join yarn C into ch2 corner sp, of your front square piece. (Make sure the flower is facing the way you want it to).

Row 1 ch3, 1tr into each st until end, 3XL move onto right side tab.

SIZES 4XL & 5XL ONLY
Row 2 ch3 and turn, 1tr into each st until end, 4XL move onto right side tab.

SIZE 5XL ONLY
Row 3 ch3 and turn, 1tr into each st until end, 5XL move onto right side tab.

Left side

SIZES 3XL, 4XL & 5XL ONLY
With your work wrong side facing front, join yarn C into opposite ch2 corner sp you joined previously.

Repeat the same steps as 'front right side tab' then move onto 'left side tab'.

Repeat side tabs on your back square.

Right side tab

With your work right side facing front, join yarn C into bottom right ch2 corner sp, of your front square. Sizes 3XL, 4XL & 5XL continue from adding width, turn your work and complete rows 1-3.

TIP
- Make sure the flower is facing the way you want it to.

Row 1 ch3, (counts as first tr throughout) 1tr into next 18 (22, 25, 31, 34, 38, 40, 42, 41) sts.

Rows 2-3 ch3 and turn, 1tr into each st until end; **repeat for row 3, then fasten off.** 19 (23, 26, 32, 35, 39, 41, 43, 42 tr)

Left side tab

With your work wrong side facing front, join yarn C into opposite ch2 corner sp you joined previously. Sizes 3XL, 4XL & 5XL continue from adding width, turn your work and complete rows 1-3.
Repeat rows 1-3 of front right side tab.
Repeat side tabs on your back square.

Front - Right top tab

With your work facing front, join yarn C into top right ch2 corner sp, of your front square. Sizes 3XL, 4XL & 5XL join into top of tr st from previous round, work 2tr sts into the side post of a tr st.

Row 1 ch3 (counts as first tr throughout), 1tr into next 8(9, 11, 14, 18, 19, 23, 26, 28) sts.

Row 2 ch3 and turn, tr2tog, then 1tr into each st until end.

Row 3 ch3 and turn, 1tr into next 5(6, 8, 11, 15, 16, 20, 23, 25) sts, then tr2tog. **Fasten off.**

Front - Left top tab

With your work wrong side facing, join yarn C into the top right ch2 corner sp of your front square. Sizes 3XL, 4XL & 5XL join into top of tr st from previous round, work 2tr sts into the side post of a tr st.
Repeat rows 1-3 of front right top tab.

Back - Right top tab

With your work facing front, join yarn C into top right ch2 corner sp, of your back square. Sizes 3XL, 4XL & 5XL join into top of tr st from previous round, work 2tr sts into the side post of a tr st.

Row 1 ch3, 1tr into each st, 1tr into ch2 sp. (31, 35, 39, 47, 55, 59, 67, 75, 79 tr)

Row 2 ch3 and turn, 1tr into each st till end.

Row 3 ch3 and turn, 1tr into next 6 (7, 9, 12, 16, 17, 21, 24, 26) sts, **fasten off**.

Back - Left top tab

With your work facing the front join yarn 7 (8, 10, 13, 17, 18, 22, 25, 27) sts to the right of the top row of sts. For sides 3XL, 4XL & 5XL, the side post of a tr st counts as 2 sts.

Row 1 ch3, 1tr into each st till end, **fasten off**. Put the front and back pieces together wrong side facing and sew up the side tabs and the top tabs with a mattress stitch, matching the sts.

Adding length

SIZE XS, S, M & L ONLY
Using yarn C, join yarn into any st along the bottom edge (I suggest joining at the side to hide the join).

TIP
- *Do 2tr into the side post of a tr st and a ch sp counts as a stitch.*

Round 1 ch3, 1tr into each st around, ss into beg ch3 to join. (86, 94, 102, 118 tr)

Round 2 cch3 and turn, 1tr into each st around, ss into beg ch3 to join. Repeat round 2 until 8 (7, 4, 2) rounds have been worked, then continue onto hem.

Hem

Using a 5mm hook and yarn C, join yarn into any st around the hem (I suggest joining at the side to hide the join). Sizes XS, S, M & L continue from previous round, turn if needed, so you are working right side facing front.

TIP
- *Do 2dc into the side post of a tr st and a ch sp counts as a stitch.*

Round 1 ch1, 1dc into each st around, ss into beg dc to join. (86, 94, 102, 118, 134, 142, 158, 174, 182 dc).

Round 2 ch1 (doesn't count as first tr), 1tr into each st around, ss into beg tr to join. (86, 94, 102, 118, 134, 142, 158, 174, 182 tr)

TIP
- *You will have the same number of stitches for the whole hem.*

Rounds 3-4 ch1, (skip ch1 from previous round), fptr into each st around, ss into beg tr to join; repeat for round 4.

Round 5 ch1, 1dc into each st around, ss into beg dc to join, **fasten off.**

COSY WINTER VIBES

Sleeve

Using a 7mm hook, join yarn C into any stitch around the armhole (I like to do it on the bottom, side seam so it is less visible).

TIP
- Do 2dc into the side post of a tr st and a ch sp counts as a stitch.

Round 1 ch1, 1dc into each st around the arm hole, ss into beg dc to join. (48, 48, 50, 54, 64, 64, 68, 72, 74 dc).

TIP
- You will have the same number of stitches for the whole sleeve.

Round 2 ch3 and turn, 1tr into each st around, ss into top of beg ch3 to join. Repeat round 2 until you have 29 (29, 29, 30, 30, 30, 30, 30, 30) rounds then continue onto the cuff.

Cuff

Change to a 5mm hook, when chaining 1 turn if needed so your work is right side facing front.

Round 1 ch1 (doesn't count as first st throughout), dc2tog around, ss into beg dc to join. (24, 24, 25, 27, 32, 32, 34, 36, 37 dc).

Round 2 ch1, 1tr into each st around, ss into beg tr to join. (24, 24, 25, 27, 32, 32, 34, 36, 37 tr).

Round 3-6 ch1, (skip ch1 from previous round), 1fptr into each sts around, ss into beg tr to join, **fasten off after round 6.**

Repeat sleeve and cuff on other side for the 2nd sleeve.

Neck

Using a 5mm hook, join yarn C into any stitch around the neck hole. (I suggest joining on the side to hide the join).

TIP

- Do 2dc sts into the side of a tr st.

Round 1 ch1 (doesn't count as first st throughout), 1dc into each st around, ss into beg dc to join. (46, 50, 50, 54, 54, 58, 58, 62, 62 dc).

TIP

. You will have the same number of stitches throughout the neck.

Round 2 ch1, 1tr into each st around, ss into beg tr to join.

Rounds 3-4 ch1, (skip ch1 from previous round), 1fptr into each st around, ss into beg tr to join.

Round 5 ch1, 1dc into each st around, ss into beg dc to join, **fasten off.**

Sew in any ends, block your finished piece and you are done.

COSY WINTER VIBES 133

SKILL LEVEL

Mittens

You need these mittens for winter! Keep those hands warm while you are out and about in the cold.

You will need:
- 6mm hook (or corresponding hook to reach gauge)
- Chunky, acrylic yarn - approx 95g total
- Brush (optional)

Recommended yarn
Stylecraft Special, chunky, acrylic

Yarn A Pistachio 30g
Yarn B Blush Pink 35g
Yarn C Washed Teal 30g

Any chunky yarn will work for this project (Yarn quantities are based on average requirements for the yarn suggested and are therefore approximate measurements.)

Tension/gauge
10cm X 10cm = 12tr sts X 7tr rows

Finished measurements
25cm X 10cm

THIS PATTERN IS WRITTEN WITH U.K. TERMS
(Key: U.K. terms)

Ch = chain
Sp = space
St = stitch
Ss = slip stitch
Dc = double crochet
Tr = treble crochet
Tr2tog = treble crochet 2 together
Tr3tog = treble crochet 3 together
... = repeat instructions
Beg = beginning

It is up to you when you change yarn colour (if you do at all) so this won't be included in the instructions.

To change yarn colour fasten off at the end of the round and rejoin the new colour. If you want the pattern to be beginner friendly, follow the pattern as instructed.

Intermediate - *However, if you want to avoid getting a line where the rounds start and end, (especially if you are changing yarn colour after each round) instead of doing ch3 as your first tr stitch, start each round with a standing tr stitch (this will count as your first tr st). Also at the end of each round when fastening off, using an invisible join.*

Mitten
Using yarn A, make a magic ring.

Round 1 ch3 (counts as first tr throughout) 11tr into ring, ss into beg ch3 to join. (12tr)

Round 2 ch3, 1tr into stitch as base of ch3, 2tr into each st around, ss into beg ch3 to join. (24tr)

Rounds 3-10 ch3, 1tr into each st around, ss into beg ch3 to join. (24tr)

Round 1

Round 2

Round 3

Round 10

TIP
- *You may want to try on the mitten at this point. It should fit comfortably over your fingers and sit just above your thumb. If you find they are too big reduce the number of rows or if they are too small increase the number of rows.*

Round 11 ch3, 1tr into next 10 sts, ch6, skip next 2 sts, then 1tr into next 11sts, ss into beg ch3 to join. (22tr +6ch)

Round 12 ch3, 1tr into next 10 sts, 1tr into each ch, 1tr into next 11 sts, ss into beg ch3 to join. (28tr)

Round 13 ch3, 1tr into each st around, ss into beg ch3 to join. (28tr)

Round 14 ch3, 1tr into next st, tr2tog, *1tr into next 2 sts, tr2tog; repeat from * around until end, ss into beg ch3 to join. (21tr)

Check your mitten fits before moving on to round 11.

Round 11 - You have just created the thumb hole.

Round 14 - Time to move onto the cuff.

Cuff

TIP
- You will be creating a slip stitch ribbing for the cuff. To make this easier you want to keep your stitches loose or you may find going up a hook size is helpful.

Ribbing

The ribbing is worked in rows off round 14.

Using yarn C, join into any st from round 14.

Row 1 ch9, ss into 2nd st from hook, ss into next 7 ch, ss into next 2 sts from round 14. (10ss)

Row 2 Turn your work, then skip 2ss, 1ss into backloop only of next 8ss. (8ss)

Row 3 ch1 and turn (doesn't count as first st), 1ss into backloop only of next 8ss, ss into next 2 sts from round 14. (10ss)

Repeat rows 2–3 until all sts from round 14 have been worked into.

Crochet the ends of the ribbing together then **fasten off**.

Thumb

Join yarn C into bottom, far right ch of thumb hole.

TIP
- If you are left handed, join yarn into far left ch.

Round 1 ch3 (counts as first tr throughout), 1tr into next 5 ch, 2tr into the side of the tr st, 1tr into same st as the tr from mittens, 1tr into next 2 sts, 1tr into same st as the tr from mittens, 2tr into the side of the tr st, ss into beg ch-3 to join. (14tr)

Work 6tr along the bottom, 2 up the side, 4 along the back and 2 down the other side, total 14tr.

Rounds 2-4 ch3, 1tr into each st around, ss into beg ch3 to join.(14tr)

Round 5 ch3, tr2tog 5 times, then tr3tog, ss into beg ch3 to join, **fasten off.** (7tr)
Leave a long enough tail to sew the top of the thumb together.

Make a second mitten in the same way.

Sew in your ends and you are all done.

Brush out the yarn (optional)
Using a mohair brush, brush out the yarn so it gives a fluffy look.

The Wally hat

SKILL LEVEL

Everyone needs a cosy hat when the weather gets cold. This hat uses just one stitch, so it is simple and fun to make.

You will need:
- 6mm hook (or corresponding hook to reach gauge)
- Aran yarn

Recommended yarn
Yarn option 1 - Stylecraft Special, aran acrylic
Yarn A Cloud Blue 75g/150m
Yarn B Dark Brown 60g/120m

Yarn option 2 - Drops Air, aran mix
Yarn A Electric Orange 50g/150m
Yarn B Crimson Red 40g/120m

Any aran yarn will work for this pattern. Using different yarn than suggested may affect the amount needed and tension. *(Yarn quantities are based on average requirements for the yarn suggested and are therefore approximate measurements.)*

Tension/gauge
10cm X 10cm = 13 sts X 12 rows of fptr

Finished measurements
52cm around, 21cm in length

THIS PATTERN IS WRITTEN WITH U.K. TERMS
(Key: U.K. terms)

Ch = chain
Sp = space
St = stitch
Ss = slip stitch
Tr = treble crochet
fptr = front post treble crochet
... = repeat instructions
Beg = beginning

Construction
This hat is worked in the round from the top down. You will be working right side facing front until you do the brim, where you will turn once (on round 24). The hem of the hat folds up to create the brim.

Front post treble crochet (fptr)

This pattern uses a fptr stitch throughout. To do a fptr stitch, wrap the yarn around your hook, insert your hook behind the treble stitch post (from front to back, then back to front, so the post is in front of the hook). Yarn over, pull up a loop around the post of the stitch, *yarn over, pull through 2 loops* twice.

Hat

You will be changing yarn colour every 2 rounds until round 21. Rounds 21-24 are worked with yarn A. After this continue to change yarn colour every 2 rounds.

TIP
- *To change the yarn colour, fasten off yarn at the end of the round and rejoin the new yarn into the first stitch from previous round.*

Using yarn A, make a magic ring.

Round 1 ch1 (doesn't count as first st throughout), 12tr into ring, ss into beg tr to join. (12tr)

Round 2 ch1, 2fptr into each st around, ss into beg fptr to join, **fasten off, change to yarn B. (24fptr)**

Round 1

Round 2

Round 3 ch1, *1fptr into next st, 2fptr into next st; repeat from * around, ss into beg fptr to join. (36fptr)

Round 4 ch1, *1fptr into next 2 sts, 2fptr into next st; repeat from * around, ss into beg fptr to join, **fasten off, change to yarn A**. (48fptr)

Round 5 ch1, *1fptr into next 3 sts, 2fptr into next st; repeat from * around, ss into beg fptr to join. (60fptr)

Round 6-23 ch1, 1fptr into each st around, ss into beg fptr to join. (60fptr)

Continue to change yarn colour every 2 rounds until round 21. Rounds 21-24 are worked with yarn A. After this continue to change yarn colour every 2 rounds.

Brim
TIP
- You will turn your work on round 24, rounds 23-30 fold up to create the brim of the hat. Don't turn on any other rounds.

Round 24 ch1 and turn, 1fptr into each st around, ss into beg fptr to join. (60fptr)

Rounds 25-30 ch1, 1fptr into each st around, ss into beg fptr to join, **Fasten off after round 30**. (60fptr)

Sew in your ends and you are all done!

What better place to wear your crocheted pieces than at a festival! These patterns are full of colour and have everything you need to get ready for the festival season.

Festival ready

SKILL BUILDER

Joining pieces together/ joining as you go

There are lots of different ways to join granny squares, but my favourite has to be the 'join as you go' method. It saves so much time and looks cute too.

Step 2

Step 4

Join as you go

1. Crochet your first square up to the round before the last round. (square 1)
2. With your next square (square 2) start the final round, leaving the corner unfinished. (Your corner should be 3tr, ch2, 3tr). Stop after the first 3tr.
3. ch1, ss into the adjoining corner of 'square 1'. Finish corner as usual with 3tr.
4. ss into next ch-1 space of 'square 1' *3tr as usual into 'square 2', ss into next ch-1 space of 'square 1'; repeat as many times as needed until you are at the ch-2 corner sp.

SKILL BUILDER

Step 5

Step 6

5   3tr into the corner space of 'square 2', ss into the adjoining corner of 'square 1', ch1, finish corner as usual with 3tr.

6   Finish square as you normally would. **Fasten off**.

Attaching on 2 sides

1. Repeat the same steps as before for one side.
2. When you get to the second corner of the square, 3tr as usual, then ss into the corner of the square above, then ss into the corner of the square to the left.
3. Finish the other side of the square, joining as you go like before.
4. Finish the square like you normally would, **fasten off**.

Step 2

Step 4

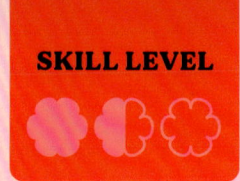

SKILL LEVEL

Mini skirt

A crocheted mini skirt is perfect for any festival. Wear with some chunky boots and a basic tee for a cool girl festival fit.

You will need:
- 5mm hook (or corresponding hook to reach gauge)
- Aran, cotton yarn

Recommended yarn
Yarn and Colors Epic cotton yarn
Yarn A   Cardinal
Yarn B   Cream
Yarn C   Ice Blue

Tension/gauge
The skirt is made from granny squares. It is important to get the size of the squares correct so the size is. Change your hook size accordingly.

Granny square after round 3 = 9.5cm X 9.5cm (after blocking)
10cm X 10cm of tr stitch = 10 sts X 6 rows (after blocking)

THIS PATTERN IS WRITTEN WITH U.K. TERMS
(Key: U.K. terms)

Ch = chain
Sp = space
St = stitch
Ss = slip stitch
Dc = double crochet
Tr = treble crochet
Tr2tog = treble crochet 2 together
... = repeat instructions
Beg = beginning

TIP
- *I would recommend blocking your squares before constructing the skirt.*

Sizing

This skirt is a mini skirt designed to sit just below your waist. The length can be altered to make longer or shorter if desired.

	XS	S	M	L	XL	2XL	3XL	4XL	5XL
To fit hips (cm)	83.5-86	89-91.5	96.5-101.5	106.5-111.5	116.5-122	132-134.5	137-139.5	142-144.5	155-157
Finished circumference of middle of skirt, once blocked (cm)	85.5	95	104.5	114	123.5	133	142.5	152	161.5
Length of skirt, once blocked (cm)	37	37	37	38.5	38.5	40	40	41.5	41.5

Yarn quantities

Quantities for each size are shown in the table. They are based on average requirements when using Yarn and Colors Epic cotton yarn and are therefore approximate measurements. Other yarns will work but it may effect the amount of yarn needed. Cotton yarn is recommended to help with the drape of the skirt.

	XS	S	M	L	XL	2XL	3XL	4XL	5XL
Total yarn	320g/480m	340g/510m	360g/540m	380g/570m	415g/623m	435g/653m	455g/683m	485g/728m	505g/758m
Yarn A	50g/75m	50g/75m	50g/75m	50g/75m	65g/98m	65g/98m	65g/98m	75g/113m	75g/113m
Yarn B	120g/180m	130g/195m	140g/210m	150g/225m	160g/240m	170g/255m	180g/270m	190g/285m	200g/300m
Yarn C	150g/225m	160g/240m	170g/255m	180g/270m	190g/285m	200g/300m	210g/315m	220g/330m	230g/345m

Skirt construction

You will make a band of granny squares (amount of granny squares used depends on size). You will then work on top of the band to create the waist and the bottom of the band to create the hem.

I would recommend blocking your individual granny squares before assembly so you have the correct size. I would then block the skirt again after construction.

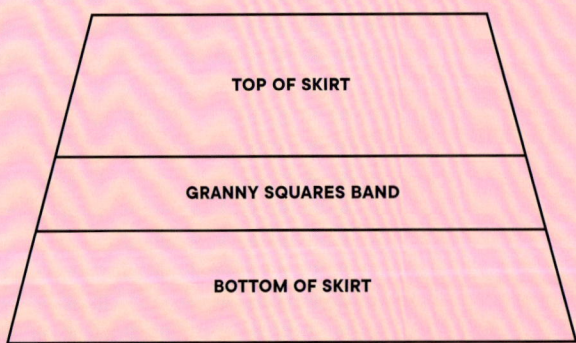

Granny square

Using yarn A, make a magic ring.

Round 1 ch3 (counts as first tr throughout), 1tr into ring, ch1, (2tr, ch1) into ring 7 times, ss into beg ch3 to join, **fasten off**. (16tr)

Round 2 join yarn B into any ch1 sp, ch3, 2tr into ch1 sp at base of ch3, ch1, (3tr, ch1) into each ch1 sp, ss into beg ch3 to join, **fasten off**. (24tr)

Round 3 join yarn C into any ch1 sp, ch3, (2tr, ch2, 3tr) into same ch1 sp, ch1, (3tr, ch1) into next ch1 sp, *(3tr, ch2, 3tr) into next ch1 sp, ch1, (3tr, ch1) into next ch1 sp; repeat from * 2 more times, then ss into beg ch3 to join, **fasten off**.

Make 9 (10, 11, 12, 13, 14, 15, 16, 17) squares up to round 3.

Joining granny squares

Now join all the granny squares needed for your size using a flat ss seam to create a band.

Round 1

Round 2

Round 3

FESTIVAL READY

Flat slip stitch seam

Using yarn A, working through just the inside loops of each st with your squares right side facing front. Insert your hook into the back loop of the first corner st of the 'right square'. It may be helpful to lay your squares on a flat surface, keeping the yarn in between the 2 squares so it is easier to pick up.

Find the same st on the 'left square', insert your hook into the inside loop only. Yarn over and pull through all the loops on your hook. Repeat these steps along the whole length of the square.

TIP
- Each granny square side has 13 sts. This is how many sts should be included in the seam. (9tr + 4ch)

Insert your hook into the back loop (inside loop) of the stich of your right square.

Insert your hook into the back loop (inside loop) of the corresponding stitch on your left square.

Edge of granny squares

Join yarn A into any stitch along top of granny square band.

Round 1 ch1 (doesn't count as first st), 1dc into each stitch around, ss into beg dc to join, **fasten off**. (117, 130, 143, 156, 169, 182, 195, 208, 221 dc)

TIP
- Each granny squares has 13 sts.

Repeat on other side of the granny square band.

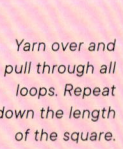

Yarn over and pull through all loops. Repeat down the length of the square.

Top of skirt

Join yarn B into any stitch along the top of the granny square band. You will be working in the round, reducing to create shape for the waist.

TIP

- When changing yarn colour travel the yarn up the inside of the skirt so you can pick it back up on the next round. Alternatively you can fasten off and join the new yarn into the first stitch from the previous round.

Round 1 ch3 (counts as first tr st), 1tr into the next 10 sts, tr2tog, *1tr into next 11 sts, tr2tog; repeat from * until end, change to yarn C, ss into top of beg ch3 to join. (108, 120, 132, 144, 156, 168, 180, 192, 204 tr)

Round 2 ch3 and turn, 1tr into the next 9 sts, tr2tog, *1tr into next 10 sts, tr2tog; repeat from * until end, change to yarn B, ss into top of beg ch3 to join. (99, 110, 121, 132, 143, 154, 165, 176, 187 tr)

Round 3 ch3 and turn, 1tr into the next 8 sts, tr2tog, *1tr into next 9 sts, tr2tog; repeat from * until end, change to yarn C, ss into top of beg ch3 to join. (90, 100, 110, 120, 130, 140, 150, 160, 170 tr)

For the following rounds, continue to change yarn colour every round.

Rounds 4–11 ch3 and turn, 1tr into each stitch around, ss into top of beg ch3 to join, change to yarn A after round 11. (90, 100, 110, 120, 130, 140, 150, 160, 170 tr)

TIP

- Turn your work if necessary so the skirt is 'right' side facing front.

Round 12 ch1 (doesn't count as first dc st), 1dc into each st around, ss into beg dc join, **fasten off**. (81, 90, 99, 108, 117, 126, 135, 144, 153 dc)

Bottom of skirt

Join yarn B into any stitch along bottom of granny square band. I suggest joining around the same place as the top of the skirt to keep the seam in the same place.

Round 1 ch3 (counts as first tr st), 1tr into the next 11 sts, 2tr into the next st, *1tr into next 12 sts, 2tr into next st; repeat from * around until end, change to yarn C, ss into top of beg ch3 to join. (126, 140, 154, 168, 182, 196, 210, 224, 238 tr)

Round 2 ch3 and turn, 1tr into the next 12 sts, 2tr into the next st, *1tr into next 13 sts, 2tr into next st; repeat from * around until end, change to yarn B, ss into top of beg ch3 to join. (135, 150, 165, 180, 195, 210, 225, 240, 255 tr)

Round 3 ch3 and turn, 1tr into the next 13 sts, 2tr into the next st, *1tr into next 14 sts, 2tr into next st; repeat from * around until end, change to yarn C, ss into top of beg ch3 to join. (144, 160, 176, 192, 208, 224, 240, 256, 272 tr)

For the following rounds continue to change yarn colour every round.

Round 4 ch3 and turn, 1tr into each stitch around, ss into top of beg ch3 to join.

Repeat round 4 until (7, 7, 7, 8, 8, 9, 9, 10, 10) rounds have been worked at bottom of skirt, then change to Yarn A.

TIP
- *If you would like the length to be longer, add more rows here.*

Hem
TIP
- *Turn your work if necessary so the skirt is 'right' side facing front.*

Round 1 ch1 (doesn't count as first dc st), 1dc into each st around, ss into beg dc join, **Fasten off**. (144, 160, 176, 192, 208, 224, 240, 256, 272 tr)

Cord/waist tie
I CORD
Pull out a length of yarn to create an extra long tail. Approx 4X the size of your waist (it is better to have pulled out too much than too little).

Leave this long tail and attach the yarn to your hook with a slip knot. *Wrap the tail of the yarn around your hook, from the front to the back. Now using the working end of the yarn, yarn over and pull through the two loops on your hook. Repeat from * until the tail end of your yarn is used up. **Fasten off.**

Alternatively, you can ch however many stitches you want your cord to be and work a dc st into each ch.

Once you have created your cord weave this in and out of the top row of tr sts. (I go in, skip 3tr stitches, come out, skip 3tr stitches; repeat.)

Block the skirt, sew in the ends and you are done!

FESTIVAL READY

SKILL LEVEL

Checked flower vest

Add some colour to your fit with this show-stopping vest!

You will need:
- 5mm hook (or corresponding hook to reach gauge)
- 4.5mm hook
- Aran, cotton yarn

Recommended yarn
Yarn and Colors Epic cotton yarn
- Merlot
- Sorbus
- Mustard
- Peony Leaf
- Lime
- Sapphire
- Thistle
- Cream
- Fawn

THIS PATTERN IS WRITTEN WITH U.K. TERMS
(Key: U.K. terms)

Ch = chain
Sp = space
St = stitch
Ss = slip stitch
Dc = double crochet
htr = half treble crochet
Tr = treble crochet
... = repeat instructions
Beg = beginning

Tension/gauge

Make sure the size of your squares matches the measurement in the table for your size. Do a test square and change your hook size accordingly. You may need to use a different hook size for the flower squares and basic squares. I recommend blocking your squares before assembling the vest to the measurements in the table.

	XS	S	M	L	XL	2XL	3XL	4XL	5XL
Square (cm) after final round	13x13	15x15	16.5x16.5	18x18	15x15	16.5x16.5	18x18	15x15	16.5x16.5

Sizing

This is a tight-fitting piece; keep this in mind when choosing which size to go for. If you want something more oversized go up a size or two. To measure your bust/chest, measure around the fullest part of your bust.

	XS	S	M	L	XL	2XL	3XL	4XL	5XL
To fit chest/Bust (cm)	71-76	81-86	91.5-96.5	101.5-106.5	111.5-117	122-127	132-137	142-147	152-158
Circumference of finished garment (cm)	78	90	99	108	120	132	144	150	165

Yarn quantities

Quantities for each size are shown in the table. They are based on average requirements when using Yarn and Colors Epic cotton yarn and are therefore approximate measurements. Other yarns will work but it may effect the amount of yarn needed.

	XS	S	M	L	XL	2XL	3XL	4XL	5XL
Total yarn	357g/570m	415g/625m	480g/725m	585g/880m	595g/895m	690g/1035m	820g/1235m	825g/1240m	875g/1315m
Yarn A (flower centres)	15g/25m	15g/25m	15g/25m	15g/25m	20g/30m	20g/30m	20g/30m	30g/45m	30g/45m
Yarn B (flower petals)	90g/135m	90g/135m	90g/135m	90g/135m	120g/180m	120g/180m	120g/180m	140g/210m	140g/210m
Yarn C (main colour of flower square-total)	85g/130m	100g/150m	125g/190m	180g/270m	135g/205m	180g/270m	245g/370m	195g/295m	210g/315m
Yarn D (solid square)	120g/180m	140g/210m	170g/255m	210g/315m	200g/300m	240g/360m	295g/445m	290g/435m	320g/480m
Yarn E (ribbing & joining)	65g/100m	70g/105m	80g/120m	90g/135m	120g/180m	130g/195m	140g/210m	170g/255m	175g/265m

Measurements

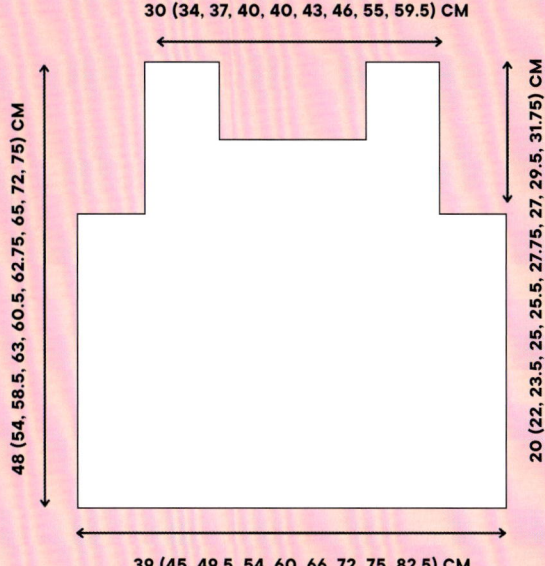

30 (34, 37, 40, 40, 43, 46, 55, 59.5) CM

48 (54, 58.5, 63, 60.5, 62.75, 65, 72, 75) CM

20 (22, 23.5, 25, 25.5, 27.75, 27, 29.5, 31.75) CM

39 (45, 49.5, 54, 60, 66, 72, 75, 82.5) CM

Vest construction

For the vest you will be making individual squares then crocheting them together to create the vest. First make the required squares for your size as described. Refer back to these diagrams showing you how to attach the squares for your size. I find it best to create the front and back pieces separately, then crochet them together along the side seams and shoulder seams. Attach the purple line with the purple line and the blue line with the blue line. The red dotted lines are fold lines.

TIP
- *Make sure are your flowers are facing the same way to keep it looking neat!*

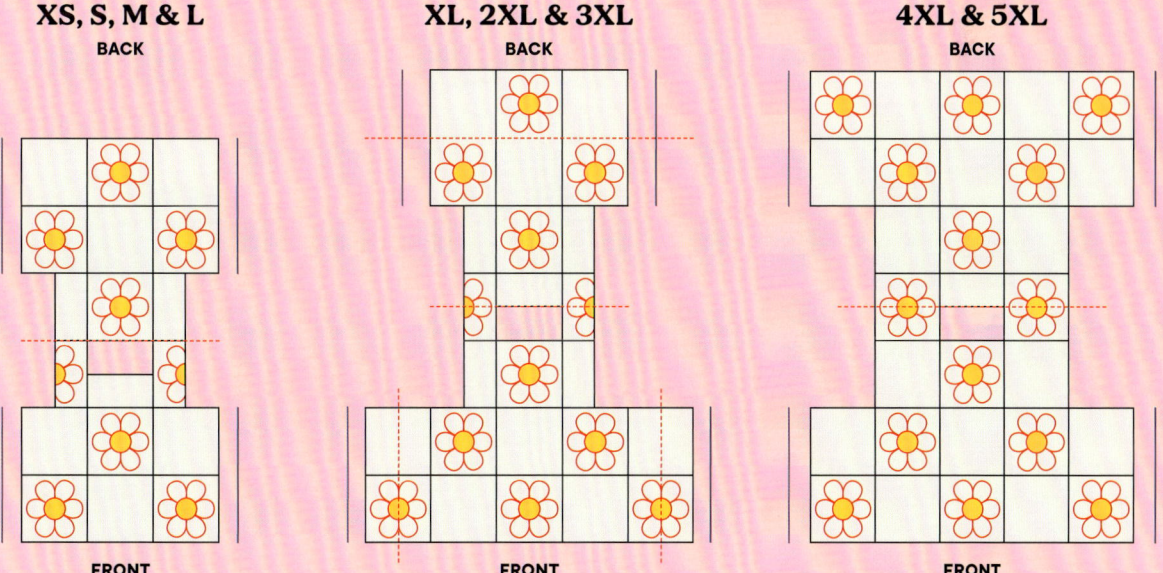

FESTIVAL READY

Flower granny square

XS, S, M & L - 7 flower squares
XL, 2XL & 3XL - 10 flower squares
4XL & 5XL - 14 flower squares

Using yarn A, make a magic ring.

Round 1 ch3 (counts as first tr throughout), 11tr into ring, ss into top of beg ch3 to join, **fasten off**. (12tr)

Round 2 Using yarn B, join yarn into any st, ch3 (counts as first tr throughout), 1tr into st at base of ch3, 1tr into next st, change to yarn C, 1tr into the same st, change to yarn B, *2tr into next st, 1tr into next st, change to yarn C, 1tr into the same st, change to yarn B; repeat from * until end ss in top beg ch3 to join. (24tr)

Round 3 ch3, 2tr into next st, 1tr in next st, change to yarn C, 2tr into next st, change to yarn B, *1tr into next st, 2tr into next st, 1tr into next st, change to yarn C, 2tr into next st, change to yarn B; repeat from * around until end, ss into top of beg ch3 to join. (36 tr)

Round 4 ch1 (doesn't count as first dc), skip st at base of ch1 and skip next st, work 5tr in between sts, skip next st, 1dc into next st, change to yarn C, 1tr into next st, 2tr into next st, *change to yarn B, 1dc into next st, skip next st, then 5tr in between sts, skip next st, 1dc into the next st, change to yarn C, 1tr into the next st, 2tr into next st; repeat from * until end, ss into beg tr to join. **Fasten off yarn B, continue with yarn C**. (60sts)

Round 5 ch3, 1tr into the stitch at base of ch3, Side 1 - ch2, 2htr into next stitch, 1htr into next 11 sts, 2htr into next st.

You will be changing yarn colour to create this design. Refer to the skill builder on pages 82-83 on how to do this.

Round 4

Made the Retro Flower Scarf yet? This pattern uses the same flower granny square (up to round 5).

Side 2 - *ch2, 2tr into next st, skip dc st, 1tr into next 3 sts, skip dc st, 1htr into next st. 1dc into next 3 sts, 1htr into next st, skip dc st, 1tr into next 3 sts,* skip dc st, 2tr into next st.

Side 3 - Repeat 'side 1'.

Side 4 - Repeat from *-* of 'side 2', then ss into beg ch3 to join.

XS ONLY
Round 6 ch1 (doesn't count as first st), 1dc into next 2 sts, *(2dc ch2, 2dc) into ch2 sp, 1dc into next 15 sts; repeat from * 2 more times, then (2dc, ch2, 2dc) into ch2 sp, 1dc into next 13 sts, ss into beg dc to join, **fasten off size**. (76dc)

S, M, L, XL, 2XL, 3XL, 4XL & 5XL ONLY
Round 6 ch3 (counts as first st), 1tr into next st, *(2tr, ch2, 2tr) into ch2 sp, 1tr into next 15 sts; repeat from * 2 more times, then (2tr, ch2, 2tr) into ch2 sp, 1tr into next 13 sts, ss into top of beg ch3 to join, **fasten off sizes S, XL & 4XL**. Continue onto round 7 for sizes M, L, 2XL, 3XL & 5XL.

M, 2XL & 5XL ONLY
Round 7 ch1 (doesn't count as first st), 1dc into next 4 sts *(2dc, ch2, 2dc) into ch2 sp, 1dc into next 19 sts; repeat from * 2 more times, then (2dc, ch2, 2dc) into ch2 sp, 1dc into next 15 sts, ss into beg dc to join, **fasten off**. (92dc)

L & 3XL ONLY
Round 7 ch3 (counts as first tr), 1tr into next 3 sts *(2tr, ch2, 2tr) into ch2 sp, 1tr into next 19 sts; repeat from * 2 more times, then (2tr, ch2, 2tr) into ch2 sp, 1tr into next 15 sts, ss into top of beg ch3 to join, **fasten off**. (92tr)

Image shows square for size S, XL & 4XL

Half flower square

XS, S, M, L, XL, 2XL & 3XL - 2 half flower squares
4XL & 5XL - 0 half flower squares

Using yarn A, make a magic ring.

Round 1 ch3 (counts as first tr throughout), 6tr into ring, **fasten off**, change to yarn C. (7tr)

Round 2 ch1 and turn (doesn't count as first st), 1tr into st at base of ch1, change to yarn B, 1tr into same st, 2tr into next st, *change to yarn C, 1tr into next st, change to yarn B, 1tr into same st, 2tr into next st; repeat from * once more, then change to yarn C, 1tr into top beg ch3. (13tr)

Round 3 ch3 and turn, 1tr into st at base of ch3, *change to yarn B, 1tr into next st, 2tr into next st, 1tr into next st, change to yarn C, 2tr into next st; repeat from * 2 more times. (20tr)

Round 4 ch3 and turn, 2tr into next st, *change to yarn B, 1dc into next st, skip next st, then work 5tr in between sts, skip next st, 1dc into next st, change to yarn C, 1tr into next st, 2tr into the next st; repeat from * 2 more times, **fasten off yarn B**, continue with yarn C. (33sts)

Round 5 ch2 and turn (counts as first htr throughout), 1htr into next 6 sts, 2htr into next st, ch2, 2tr into the next st, skip dc st, 1tr into next 3 sts, skip dc st, 1htr into next st, 1dc into next 3 sts, 1htr into next st, skip dc st, 1tr into next 3 sts, skip dc st, 2tr into next st, ch2, 2htr into next st, 1htr into next 7 sts.

166 NOT YOUR GRANDMA'S CROCHET

S ONLY
Round 6 ch1 and turn, 1dc into next 9sts, (2dc, ch2, 2dc) into ch2 sp; 1dc into next 15sts, (2dc, ch2, 2dc) into ch2 sp, 1dc into next 9sts, fasten off <make bold>. (short sides - 11dc, long side - 19dc)

S, M, L, XL, 2XL, 3XL, 4XL, 5XL ONLY
Round 6 ch3 and turn, 1tr into next 8sts, (2tr, ch2, 2tr) into ch2 sp, 1tr into next 15sts, (2tr, ch2, 2tr) into ch2 sp, 1tr into next 9sts, **fasten off sizes S, XL & 4XL**. (short sides - 11tr, long side - 19tr)

Continue onto round 7 for sizes M, L, 2XL, 3XL & 5XL.

M, 2XL & 5XL ONLY
Round 7 ch1 and turn (doesn't count as first dc), 1dc into next 11sts, (2dc, ch2, 2dc) into ch2 sp, 1dc into next 19sts, (2dc, ch2, 2dc) into ch2 sp, 1dc into next 11sts, **fasten off**. (short sides - 13dc, long side - 23dc)

L & 3XL ONLY
Round 7 ch3 and turn, 1tr into next 10sts, (2tr, ch2, 2tr) into ch2 sp, 1tr into next 19sts, (2tr, ch2, 2tr) into ch2 sp, 1tr into next 11sts, **fasten off**. (Short sides - 13tr, long side - 23tr)

Image shows half square for sizes S, XL & 4XL

FESTIVAL READY

Solid granny square

XS, S, M & L – 6 solid granny squares
XL, 2XL & 3XL – 8 solid granny squares
4XL & 5XL – 14 solid granny squares

Using yarn D, make a magic ring.
Round 1 ch3 (counts as first tr throughout), 2tr into ring, ch2, (3tr, ch2) into ring 3 times, ss into beg ch3 to join. (12tr)

Rounds 2-4 ch1 and turn, ss into ch2 sp at base of ch1, ch3, 1tr into same ch2 sp, 1tr into each st, *(2tr, ch2, 2tr) into ch2 sp, 1tr into each st; repeat from * 2 more times, then (2tr, ch2) into beg ch2 sp, ss into beg ch3 to join. (60tr)

XS/S ONLY
Round 5 ch1 and turn, ss into ch2 sp at base of ch1, ch1 (doesn't count as first dc), 2dc into same ch2 sp, 1dc into each st, *(2dc, ch2, 2dc) into ch2 sp, 1dc into each st; repeat from * 2 more times, then (2dc, ch2) into beg ch2 sp, ss into beg dc to join, **fasten off.** (76dc)

S, M, L, XL, 2XL, 3XL, 4XL, 5XL ONLY
Round 5 ch1 and turn, ss into ch2 sp at base of ch1, ch3, 1tr into same ch2 sp, 1tr into each st, *(2tr, ch2, 2tr) into ch2 sp, 1tr into each st; repeat from * 2 more times, then (2tr, ch2) into beg ch2 sp, ss into beg ch3 to join, **fasten off sizes S, XL & 4XL.** (76tr)

Continue onto round 6 for sizes M, L, 2XL, 3XL & 5XL.

M, 2XL & 5XL ONLY
Round 6 ch1 and turn, ss into ch2 sp at base of ch1, ch1 (doesn't count as first dc), 2dc into same ch2 sp, 1dc into each st, *(2dc, ch2, 2dc) into ch2 sp, 1dc into each st; repeat from * 2 more times, then (2dc, ch2) into beg ch2 sp, ss into beg dc to join, **fasten off.** (92dc)

L & 3XL ONLY
Round 6 ch1 and turn, ss into ch2 sp at base of ch1, ch3, 1tr into same ch2 sp, 1tr into each st, *(2tr, ch2, 2tr) into ch2 sp, 1tr into each st; repeat from * 2 more times, then (2tr, ch2) into beg ch2 sp, ss into beg ch3 to join, **fasten off.** (92tr)

Round 4 - all sizes

Round 5 - sizes S–5XL

Round 6- M, 2XL & 5XL

Half solid square

XS, S, M & L - 3 half solid squares
XL, 2XL & 3XL - 5 half Solid squares
4XL & 5XL - 1 half solid square

Using yarn D, make a magic ring.
Round 1 ch3 (counts as first tr throughout), 2tr into ring, *ch2, 3tr into ring; repeat from *once more.

Round 2 ch3 and turn, 1tr into next 2 sts, *(2tr, ch2, 2tr) into ch2 sp, 1tr into next 3 sts; repeat from * once more.

Round 3 ch3 and turn, 1tr into next 4 sts, (2tr, ch2, 2tr) into ch2 sp, 1tr into next 7 sts, (2tr, ch2, 2tr) into ch2 sp, 1tr into next 5 sts.

Round 4 ch3 and turn, 1tr into next 6 sts, (2tr, ch2, 2tr) into the ch2 sp, 1tr into next 11 sts, (2tr, ch2, 2tr) into ch2 sp, 1tr into next 7 sts.

XS ONLY
Round 5 ch1 (doesn't count as first dc) and turn, *1dc into next 9 sts, (2dc, ch2, 2dc) into ch2 sp, 1dc into next 15 sts, (2dc, ch2, 2dc) into ch2 sp, 1dc into next 9 sts, **fasten off**. (short sides - 11dc, long side - 19dc)

S, M, L, XL, 2XL, 3XL, 4XL & 5XL ONLY
Round 5 ch3 and turn, *1tr into next 8 sts, (2tr, ch2, 2tr) into ch2 sp, 1tr into next 15 sts, (2tr, ch2, 2tr) into ch2 sp, 1tr into next 9 sts, **fasten off sizes S, XL & 4XL**. (short sides - 11tr, long side - 19tr)

Continue onto round 6 for sizes M, L, 2XL, 3XL & 5XL.

M, 2XL & 5XL ONLY
Round 6 ch1 and turn (doesn't count as first dc), *1dc into next 11 sts, (2dc, ch2, 2dc) into the ch2 sp, 1dc into next 19 sts, (2dc, ch2, 2dc) into ch2 sp, 1dc into next 11 sts, **fasten off**. (short sides - 13dc, long side - 23dc)

L & 3XL ONLY
Round 6 ch3 and turn, *1tr into next 10 sts, (2tr, ch2, 2tr) into ch2 sp, 1tr into next 19 sts, (2tr, ch2, 2tr) into ch2 sp, 1tr into next 11 sts, **fasten off**. (short sides - 13tr, long side - 23tr)

Round 4 - all sizes

Round 5 - sizes S–5XL

Attaching the square

Attach the squares using a flat ss seam to create separate front and back pieces, in the formation shown in the diagram for your size. Once you have attached the squares in one direction, do the same thing to attach them in the opposite direction.

Now you have created the front and back pieces, you will need to add to the top 2 outer squares on each side. Don't join the front and back pieces just yet.

Flat slip stitch seam

Using yarn E, work through just the inside loops of each st with your squares right side facing front.

Insert your hook into the back loop of the first corner st of the 'right square'. Find the same st on the 'left square', insert your hook into the inside loop only. Yarn over and pull through all the loops on your hook. Repeat these steps along the whole length of the square.

Without fastening off continue onto your next set of squares in the same direction (make sure you keep a relatively loose tension, you may want to go up a hook size if you feel your tension is too tight).

Adding to the top tabs
For all sizes - except size 3XL

You will be adding length to the top tabs to make the arm holes and neck hole bigger. Working into the top 4 outer squares; 2 squares from the front piece and 2 squares from the back piece. Use the same colour yarn used for each square so the tabs match.

Join yarn into top far stitch of your first square.

Front

Back

Insert your hook into the back loop (inside loop) of the stitch of your right square.

Insert your hook into the back loop (inside loop) of the corresponding stitch on your left square.

Yarn over and pull through all loops. Repeat down the length of the square.

Rows 1-X ch3 (counts as first tr), 1tr into each st until end, **fasten off after row 2 (2, 2, 2, 1, 1, na, 2, 2).** (12, 12, 14, 14, 12, 14, na, 12, 14 tr)

TIPS
- *Do 1tr into each ch2 corner sp.*

Repeat into the other 3 squares.
Now join the top tabs and the side seams with a ss seam like before.

Ribbing
Hem
Using a 4.5mm hook attach yarn E into any st along the vests bottom hem. (I suggest at the side seam to make it neat).

The ribbing is worked in rows off the granny squares.

Row 1 ch5 (5, 5, 5, 11, 5, 5, 11, 5), 1dc into 2nd ch from hook, 1dc into each ch, ss into next 2 sts of granny squares. (4, 4, 4, 4, 10, 4, 4, 10, 4 dc + 2ss).

Row 2 Turn your work, then skip 2 ss, 1dc into backloop only of each dc st. (4, 4, 4, 4, 10, 4, 4, 10, 4 dc).

Row 3 ch1 and turn (doesn't count as first st), 1dc into backloop only of each dc st, ss into next 2 sts of granny squares. (4, 4, 4, 4, 10, 4, 4, 10, 4 dc + 2ss).

Repeat rows 2–3 until all sts from granny squares have been worked into.

Fasten off and sew the ends of the ribbing together.

Neck
Repeat ribbing around the neck, starting with ch5 for all sizes. (4dc). When working on the side of a tr stitch, work 2dc around the post of the st.

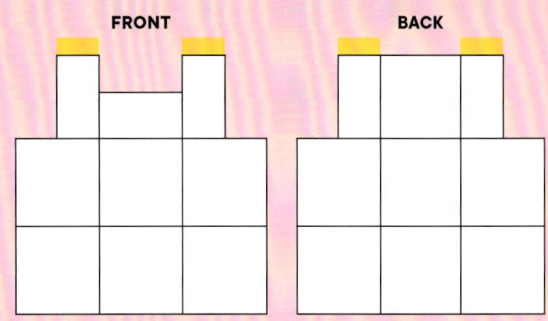

Arm Hole
Repeat the ribbing around the arm holes, stating with ch - (5, 5, 5, 5, 5,11, 11, 11, 11). (4, 4, 4, 4, 4, 10, 10, 10, 10 dc)

Sew in the end and you are all done!

Granny square hat

SKILL LEVEL

A crocheted hat is a festival essential. Make this in your favourite colours so you can be spotted by your friends in the crowd.

You will need:
- 4mm hook (or corresponding hook to reach gauge)
- DK yarn

Recommended yarn
Paintbox yarns, cotton, DK
Yarn A   Slate Green, 5g
Yarn B   Bubblegum Pink, 10g
Yarn C   Sailor Blue, 15g
Yarn D   Champagne White, 55g

Any DK yarn will work for this pattern (Yarn quantities are based on average requirements for the yarn suggested and are therefore approximate measurements.)

THIS PATTERN IS WRITTEN WITH U.K. TERMS
(Key: U.K. terms)
Ch = chain
Sp = space
St = stitch
Ss = slip stitch
Dc = double crochet
Tr = treble crochet
... = repeat instructions
Beg = beginning

Tension/gauge
Granny square (after round 4) = 10cm X 10cm

Finished measurements
21cm X 24cm (one size, adult woman)

Construction of the hat

The hat is made by creating a band of granny squares, then working onto this to create the brim. A circle is made for the top which is sewn on at the end.

Granny squares

Make 5 squares joining as you go in a strip. With the last one you will need to join the band together by joining as you go on parallel sides to create a band.

ch4, ss to first ch to join and made a ring.

Round 1 ch3 (counts as first tr), 2tr into ring, (ch2, 3tr) 3 times, ch2, ss into top of beg ch3 to join. **Fasten off.** (12tr)

Round 2 Join new colour into ch2 sp, ch3 (counts as first tr), (2tr, ch2, 3tr) in same ch2 sp, ch1, *(3tr, ch2, 3tr) into next ch2 sp, ch1; repeat from * 2 more times, ss into top of beg ch3 to join. **Fasten off.** (24tr)

Round 3 Join new colour into any ch2 sp, ch3 (counts as first tr), (2tr, ch2, 3tr) into same ch2 sp, ch1, 3tr into next ch1 sp, ch1 *(3tr, ch2, 3tr) into next ch2 sp, ch1, 3tr in next ch1 sp, ch1; repeat from * 2 more times, ss into top of beg ch3 to join. **Fasten off.** (36tr)

Round 4 (Join as you go). Join yarn D into any ch2 sp, ch3 (counts as first tr), (2tr, ch2, 3tr) into same ch2 sp, ch1, 3tr in next ch1 sp, ch1, 3tr into next ch1 sp, ch1 *(3tr, ch2, 3tr) into next ch2 sp, ch1, 3tr into next ch1 sp, ch1, 3tr into next ch1 sp, ch1; repeat from * 2 more times, ss into top of beg ch3 to join, **fasten off.** (48tr)

Round 3

Join as you go

- Crochet your first square up to round 4. (square 1)
- With your next square (square 2) start round 4, leaving the corner unfinished. (Your corner should be 3tr, ch2, 3tr.) Stop after the first 3tr.
- ch1, ss into the adjoining corner of 'square 1'. Finish the corner of square 2 as usual, with 3tr.
- ss into next ch1 space of 'square 1', *3tr as usual into 'square 2', ss into next ch1 sp of square 1. Repeat from * 1 more time.
- 3tr into ch2 corner space of 'square 2', ch1, ss into the adjoining corner of 'square 1', finish the corner as usual with 3tr.
- Finish square as you normally would.

Create the band by joining as you go on parallel sides with the last granny square.

Hat Brim

Round 1 Join yarn D into any st, ch3 (counts as first tr throughout), 1tr into st at base of ch3, 2tr into each st around until end, ss into top of beg ch3 to join. (170tr)

Rounds 2-4 ch3, 1tr into each st around, ss into beg ch3 to join, **fasten off after round 4**. (170tr)

Top edge of granny squares

Join yarn D into any st in the top of granny square band.

Round 1 ch3 (counts as first tr), 1tr into each st around, ss into top of beg ch3 to join, **fasten off**. (85tr)

TIP
- *Each square has 17 sts*

Top

Using yarn D make a magic ring.

Round 1 ch3 (counts as first tr throughout), 11tr into ring, ss into top of beg ch3 to join. (12tr)

Round 2 ch3, 1tr in st at base of ch3, 2tr into each st around, ss in top beg ch3 to join. (24tr)

Round 3 ch3, 2tr into next st, *1tr into next st, 2tr into next st; repeat from * around until end, ss into top of beg ch3 to join. (36tr)

Round 4 ch3, 1tr into next st, 2tr into next st, *1tr into next 2 sts, 2tr into next st; repeat from * around, ss into top of beg ch3 to join. (48tr)

Round 5 ch3, 1tr into next 2 sts, 2tr into next st, *1tr into next 3 sts, 2tr into next st; repeat from * around until end, ss into top of beg ch3 to join. (60tr)

Round 6 ch3, 1tr into next 3 sts, 2tr into next st, *1tr into next 4 sts, 2tr into next st; repeat from * around until end, ss into top of beg ch3 to join. (72tr)

Round 7 ch3, 1tr into st at base of ch3, 1tr into next 4 sts, 2tr into next st, *1tr into next 5 sts, 2tr into next st; repeat from * around until end, ss into top of beg ch3 to join, **fasten off**. (85tr)

TIP
- Leave a long enough tail to sew the round top to the rest of the hat.

Sewing the pieces together
Sew the 'top' to the 'top edge' of the granny square band using a mattress stitch.

Sew in your ends and you are done!

Round 7

Granny square across body bag

SKILL LEVEL

Head out for the day with your festival essentials in the granny square bag. Designed to be worn across the body so you can dance the night away.

You will need:
- 5mm hook (or corresponding hook to reach gauge)
- Aran, cotton yarn - approx. 165g

Recommended yarn
Yarn and Colors Epic, Cotton, Aran

Yarn A	Cream, 120g
Yarn B	Pepper, 5g
Yarn C	Orange Juice, 5g
Yarn D	Lime, 5g
Yarn E	Grass, 5g
Yarn F	Opaline Glass, 5g
Yarn G	Sapphire, 5g
Yarn H	Violet, 5g
Yarn I	Fuchsia, 5g
Yarn J	Cotton Candy, 5g

Any aran yarn will work for this pattern. This is a great pattern for using up scrap yarn. *(Yarn quantities are based on average requirements for the yarn suggested and are therefore approximate measurements.)*

Tension/gauge
Granny square (after round 3) = 9cm x 9cm

Finished measurements
Bag = 25cm X 26cm
Strap = 75cm

THIS PATTERN IS WRITTEN WITH U.K. TERMS
(Key: U.K. terms)

Ch = chain
Sp = space
St = stitch
Ss = slip stitch
Dc = double crochet
Tr = treble crochet
... = repeat instructions
Beg = beginning

FESTIVAL READY 179

Front

You will want to create 9 granny squares for the front of the bag. Using the joining as you go' method to attach the squares at round 3.

Granny square

Make a magic ring.

Round 1 ch4 (counts as first tr + ch1), (1tr, ch1) into ring 7 times, ss into the 3rd ch of beg ch4 to join, **fasten off**. (8tr + 8ch)

Round 2 Join new colour into any ch1 sp, ch3 (counts as first tr throughout), 2tr into same ch1 sp, (3tr, ch1) into each ch1 sp around, ss into top of beg ch3 to join, **fasten off**. (24tr + 8ch)

Round 3

Join as you go to create a 3 X 3 squares.

Round 3 (Join as you go). Join new colour in between any ch1 sp, ch3, (2tr, ch2, 3tr) into same sp, ch1, *3tr into next ch1 sp, ch1, (3tr, ch2, 3tr) into next ch1 sp, ch1; repeat from * 2 times, 3tr into next ch1 sp, ch1, ss into top of beg ch3 to join, **fasten off**. (36tr + 16ch)

Create a 3 X 3 square

Join as you go

1. Crochet your first square up to the round before the last round. (square 1)
2. With your next square (square 2) start the final round, leaving the corner unfinished. (Your corner should be 3tr, ch2, 3tr). Stop after the first 3tr.
3. ch1, ss into the adjoining corner of 'square 1'. Finish corner as usual with 3tr.
4. ss into next ch-1 space of 'square 1' *3tr as usual into 'square 2', ss into next ch-1 space of 'square 1'; repeat as many times as needed until you are at the ch-2 corner sp.

Step 2

Step 4

5   3tr into the corner space of 'square 2', ss into the adjoining corner of 'square 1', ch1, finish corner as usual with 3tr.
6   Finish square as you normally would, **fasten off**.

Step 5

Step 6

Attaching on 2 sides
1   Repeat the same steps as before for one side.
2   When you get to the second corner of the square, 3tr as usual, then ss into the corner of the square above, then ss into the corner of the square to the left.
3   Finish the other side of the square, joining as you go like before.
4   Finish the square like you normally would, **fasten off**.

Step 1

Step 2

Step 4

FESTIVAL READY 181

Back

Using yarn A, make a magic ring.

Round 1 ch3 (counts as first tr throughout), 2tr into ring, ch2, (3tr, ch2) into ring 3 times, ss into top of beg ch3 to join. (12sts)

Round 2 ch3 and turn, 2tr into ch2 sp at base of ch3, ch1, *(3tr, ch2, 3tr) into next ch2 sp, ch1; repeat from * 2 more times, (3tr, ch2) into beg ch2 sp, ss into top of beg ch3 to join. (24 sts)

Round 3 ch3 and turn, 2tr into ch2 sp at base of ch3, ch1, (3tr, ch1) into next ch1 sp, *(3tr, ch2, 3tr) into next ch2 sp, ch1, (3tr, ch1) into next ch1 sp; repeat from* 2 more times, (3tr, ch2) into beg ch2 sp, ss into top of beg ch3 to join. (36sts)

Round 3

Rounds 4-9 ch3 and turn, 2tr into ch2 sp at base of ch3, ch1, *(3tr, ch1) into each ch1 sp, (3tr, ch2, 3tr) into next ch2 sp, ch1; repeat from * 2 more times, (3tr, ch1) into each ch1 sp, (3tr, ch2) into beg ch2 sp, ss into beg ch3 to join, **fasten off after round 9.** (108sts at end of Round 9)

Round 9

Block

At this point block the front and back pieces so they are 25cm X 25cm.

Attaching front and back

Sew together the front and back pieces, along 3 sides. Right sides together, matching up the stitches, using a whip stitch.

TIP

- When matching the front and back pieces, match a chain with a chain and a treble st with a treble st. You will need to go through the back ch st twice at the point where 2 squares join on the front so the stitches match up.

Top edge of bag

Working on the front piece, join yarn A into the 2nd tr st from the right

Row 1 ch1 (doesn't count as first dc), 1dc into each st around, ss into top beg dc to join. (76dc)

TIP
- *Each small square has 13 sts (x3 = 39). Back has 36 sts plus corner spaces across top edge*

Row 2 ch3 (counts as first tr), 1tr into each st around, ss into beg ch3 to join, **fasten off**. (76tr)

Strap

Rows 1-45 ch3 and turn, 1tr into next 5 sts, **fasten off after row 45**. (6tr)

TIP
- *Leave a long enough tail to sew the strap onto the other side.*

Sew the other end of the strap to the opposite side.

Sew in your ends and you are done!

Index

Note: page numbers in **BOLD** refer to illustrations.

A
arms, ribbing 66, **66**, 171
attaching on 2 sides 27, **27**, 61, **61**, 151, **151**, 181, **181**

B
bags
   Daisy chain 100, **101–7**, 102–7
   Granny square across body 178, **179–183**, 180–3
   Hold my ruffle 94, **94–9**, 96–9
   linings 107, **107**
   Retro flower 72, **73–7**, 74–7
blocking 113, 182
Bookmark 16, **17–19**, 18–19
brims, hat 143, **143**, 176, **176**
brushing out yarn 139
buttons 31

C
cardigan, Granny squares & stripes 20, **21**, 22–31, **23–31**
chain (ch) 47, **47**
Checked flower vest 160, **161–171**, 162–171
Coasters 12, **13–15**, 14–15
collar, Granny stripe 50, **51–5**, 52–5
colour changes 14–15, **14–15**, 82–3, **83**
   Mini skirt 157
   Mittens 136, **136**
   Raglan short sleeved jumper 35, **35**
   Retro flower bag 74
   Retro flower jumper 124
   Retro flower scarf 116
   Summer flower top hat 90
   Wally hat 142, **142**
cords 87, **87**, 159, **159**
cuffs 31, **31**, 132, **132**, 138, **138**

D
Daisy chain bag 100, **101–7**, 102–7
double crochet (dc) 47, **47**
double crochet 2 together (dc2tog) 48, **48**
double treble crochet (dtr) 48, **48**

E
edging 55
   raw 65–66
elastic 68, **70**, 71
ends, sewing in 113

F
fastenings 55
   cords 87, **87**, 159, **159**
   see also buttons
finishing pieces 112–13
flat slip stitch seam 156, **156**, 170, **170**

floral designs
    Bookmark 16, **17–19**, 18–19
    Checked flower vest 160, **161–171**, 162–171
    Coaster 12, **13–15**, 14–15
    Daisy chain bag 100, **101–7**, 102–7
    Retro flower bag 72, **73–7**, 74–7
    Retro flower jumper 120, **121–33**, 122–33
    Retro flower scarf 114, **114–19**, 116–19
    Summer flower top hat 88, **89–93**, 90–3
front post treble crochet (fptr) 49, **49**, 142, **142**

G

gauge/tension 11
    Bookmark 16
    Checked flower vest 162
    Coaster 12
    Daisy chain bag 100
    Grandad's vest 58
    Granny square across body bag 178
    Granny square hat 172
    Granny squares & stripes cardigan 22
    Granny stripe collar 50
    Hold my ruffle bag 96
    Love heart scrunchie 68
    Mini skirt 152
    Mittens 134
    Raglan short sleeved jumper 32
    Retro flower bag 72
    Retro flower jumper 122
    Retro flower scarf 114
    Summer flower top hat 88
    Sunglasses case 84
    Wally hat 140
gauge swatches 11, 96, **96**
Grandad's vest 56, **57**, 58–67, **59–67**
granny squares 59, **59**, 60–1, **60–1**
    blocking 113
    Checked flower vest 164–171, **164–171**
    edge of 156, **156**, 176, **176**
    flower 116–18, **116–18**
    Granny square across body bag 178, **179–183**, 180–3
    Granny square hat 172, **173–177**, 174–177
    Granny squares & stripes cardigan 20, **21**, 22–31, **23–31**
    joining 87, **87**, 155–156, **155–156**
    Mini skirt 154–157, **154–157**
    Retro flower jumper 124–7, **125–7**
    Sunglasses case 86–7, **86–7**
Granny stripe collar 50, **51–5**, 52–5
granny stripe stitch 29
granny triangles 59, **59**, 64–5, **64–5**

H

half flower squares 166–167, **166–167**
half granny squares 59, **59**, 62–3, **62–3**
half solid squares 169, **169**
half treble crochet (htr) 48, **48**

hats
  brims 143, **143**, 176, **176**
  Granny square hat 172, **173-177**, 174–177
  Summer flower top hat 88, **89-93**, 90–3
  Wally hat 140, **141-3**, 142–3
  wire 93, **93**
hem ribbing 39, **39**, 40, **40**, 171
  Grandad's vest 67, **67**
hems
  cardigan 31
  jumper 131, **131**
  Mini skirt 158
Hold my ruffle bag 94, **94-9**, 96–9

I
I CORD 159, **159**

J
joining
  flowers 103, **103**
  granny squares 87, **87**, 155–156, **155-156**
  granny triangles 65, **65**
  half squares 63, **63**
  'join as you go' method 26, **26**, 39–40, **39-40**, 60, **60**, 86, **86**, 148–151, **149-151**, 175, **175**, 180–1, **180-1**
jumpers
  Raglan short sleeved 32, **33-41**, 34–41
  Retro flower 120, **121-33**, 122–33

L
leaf designs 19, **19**
length, adding 130, **130**, 158
linings, bag 107, **107**
Love heart scrunchie 68, **69-71**, 71

M
magic rings
  Bookmark 18, **18**
  Checked flower vest 164, **164**, 166, **166**, 169, **169**
  Coaster 15, **15**
  Granny square across body bag 180, **180**, 182, **182**
  Granny square hat 176, **176**
  Mini Skirt 155, **155**
  Mittens 136, **136**
  Retro Flower Bag 74–6, **74-6**
  Retro flower jumper 124, **125**
  Retro flower scarf 116, **116**
  Summer flower top hat 91, **91**
  Sunglasses case 86, **86**
  Wally hat 142–3, **142-3**
mattress stitch 119
Mini skirt 152, 153–159, 154–159
Mittens 134, **135-9**, 136–9

N
necks
  Grandad's vest 66, **66**
  Retro flower jumper 133, **133**
  ribbing 41, **41**, 66, **66**, 171

R
Raglan short sleeved jumper 32, **33-41**, 34–41
'raw' edges 65–6
Retro flower bag 72, **73-7**, 74–7
Retro flower jumper 120, **121-33**, 122–33
Retro flower scarf 114, **114-19**, 116–19
ribbed stitch 39–41, **39-41**
ribbing
  arms 66, **66**, 171

cuff 138, **138**
hem 39, **39**, 40, **40**, 67, **67**, 171
necks 41, **41**, 66, **66**, 171
slip stitch 138, **138**

S
scarf, Retro flower 114, **114–19**, 116–19
scrunchie, Love heart 68, **69–71**, 71
sewing in ends 113
sizing 11
    Checked flower vest 162–163, **163**, 164–171, **165**, **167**
    Grandad's vest 58
    Granny squares & stripes cardigan 22–25, 30–1
    Mini skirt 152, **152**, 158
    Mittens 137, **137**
    Raglan short sleeved jumper 34
    Retro flower jumper 122–3, **122–3**, 128, **128**, 130, **130**
skirt, Mini 152, 153–159, 154–159
sleeves
    Granny squares & stripes cardigan 22–3, **22**, 29–30, **30**
    Raglan short sleeved jumper 34, **34**, 40, **40**
    Retro flower jumper 132, **132**
slip knots 47, **47**
slip stitch (ss) 47, **47**, 138, **138**
steaming 113
stems 18, **18**
stitch directory 46–9
straps 76, **76**, 96–7, **97**, 106, **106**, 183, **183**
striped designs
    Granny squares & stripes cardigan 20–31, **21**, **23–31**
    Granny stripe collar 50, **51–5**, 52–5

Summer flower top hat 88, **89–93**, 90–3
Sunglasses case 84, **85–7**, 86–7
synthetic fibres 113

T
tabs 129–30, **129–30**, 170–171, **170–171**
tension see gauge/tension
terminology 11
thumbs 138–9, **138–9**
treble crochet (tr) 48, **48**
treble crochet 2 together (tr2tog) 49, **49**

V
vests
    Checked flower 160, **161–171**, 162–171
    Grandad's 56, **57**, 58–67, **59–67**

W
waist ties 159, **159**
Wally hat 140, **141–3**, 142–3
width, adding 128, **128**
wire, hat 93, **93**

Y
yarn
    brushing out 139
    changing see colour changes
yokes 34–7, **34–6**